Grammar Made Easy

Grammar Made Easy

Jose K . C

authorHOUSE®

AuthorHouse™
1663 Liberty Drive
Bloomington, IN 47403
www.authorhouse.com
Phone: 1-800-839-8640

Published by AuthorHouse   02/28/2012

ISBN: 978-1-4567-9631-0 (sc)
ISBN: 978-1-4567-9632-7 (e)

Any people depicted in stock imagery provided by Thinkstock are models, and such images are being used for illustrative purposes only.
Certain stock imagery © Thinkstock.

This book is printed on acid-free paper.

Because of the dynamic nature of the Internet, any web addresses or links contained in this book may have changed since publication and may no longer be valid. The views expressed in this work are solely those of the author and do not necessarily reflect the views of the publisher, and the publisher hereby disclaims any responsibility for them.

PREFACE

In the process of mastering the use of English, it is advisable to club the twin approaches—'learn English to use it' and 'use English to learn it.' In both the L1 and L2 situations—especially in the latter—we had better study grammar and its beautiful nuances in usage. This is all the more resoundingly true with teachers of English. Who is better qualified as a trustworthy physician—one who simply but rightly prescribes the right medicines out of experience or one who does so after a study of the anatomy, physiology and pharmacology etc., besides experience?

Just as a gymnast, after (isolated) exercises in his/her gym, has enough flexibility, stamina and strength to lift a bucket of water to re-position it in the kitchen, even isolated grammar exercises make one linguistically flexible and strong. These exercises give the weak as well as the physician, who attends on the weak, added confidence in life.

'Grammar Made Easy' is made in that philosophy and is useful to High School Plus users, the teachers and the college lecturers. Grammar in the book is contextualized in simple tales—a sort of language through literature.

*   *   *   *   *

The passionate seeds of grammar were sown in me in Level VIII by Sr. Emerita and Sr. Jacob. It grew well as I explained grammar daily to my school mates on our one-hour walk home in the evenings along the road not taken and less travelled by day scholars.

Later, the grammar fire rekindled to a good flame when I met my college mates, Mr. Sojan Jose and Mr. (now Dr.) Joy George with whom I often had long discussion sessions on language uses.

Now, I am convinced that grammar is pleasant to learn when rightly approached. The uncharitable label 'dry' on grammar is incomprehensible. After all, he who loves something is its master; he who hates it is its slave.

Hope this book would make masters, language lovers and thus culture custodians.

JOSE KC

CONTENTS

1. SUBJECT-VERB AGREEMENT

1.1 ONE OF THE HARES IS CLEVER (CONCORD-1)

A large herd of elephants lives in a green, peaceful land. But soon, times turn bad. There is no rain for twelve years. Twelve years is not a matter of joke. One day, the smallest of the elephants dies. The pain at the death is too much for them. The king of the herd, Four Tusks, orders his herd to march to the distant Lake of the Moon.

While marching along the bank of the Lake, the elephants crush the many hares that live there. The excited elephants jump into the lake and perform gymnastics in the water. Gymnastics is alright. But their sport disturbs and even kills many of the hares.

A meeting of the hares are divided in their ideas as to what to do. At last, the meeting decides to ask Jeet, the cleverest of the hares, to talk to Four Tusks. Jeet goes and says, "O, great king of the elephants, may I have a word with you?" Jeet's flattery pleases Four Tusks. "The Moon God of the Lake," Jeet continues, "is angry with you all because you make his lake dirty. The God says, 'Either Four Tusks or I win, not both.'"

Four Tusks is really scared. His herd goes away. Every hare applauds Jeet's bravery. The means Jeet has used to chase away the herd is clever, they say.

All the words underlined above are the main verbs in those sentences. And most of them('lives', 'is', 'is' 'dies', 'is', 'orders', 'is', 'disturbs', 'decides', 'pleases', 'goes', 'applauds', 'has' and 'is') end in 's'. The other verbs (turn', 'crush', 'live', 'are', 'make', 'win') don't end in 's'.

Remember: Generally, Verbs with 'S'—ending are **S**ingular.
(Nouns with 'S'—ending are Plural.)

In other words, the singular verbs above agree with the singular noun-subjects in the third person. This 'singular subject – singular verb/ plural subject –plural verb' agreement is called concord.

Jose K . C

Let's consider the sentences one by one:

1. A large herd of elephants lives in a green, peaceful land. (*'A herd'* is a collective noun. Collective nouns take a singular verb)
2. At last, the meeting decides to ask Jeet, . . . (*'meeting'* is another collective noun; hence the singular verb, *'decides'*)
3. Some of the other collective nouns are: *a group (of things), a crowd (of people), a tuft/lock (of hair), a flock (of sheep), herd (of cattle/elephants), a congregation (of worshippers), a constellation/ galaxy (of stars), a fleet (of ships), the committee, the council, the parliament, the public, the audience, the army, the crew and the police etc.*

However, when individuals in the collective nouns are in mind, then even collective nouns take plural verbs. That is why, the story has:

4. A meeting of the hares are divided in their ideas as to what to do. (Here, the individuals in the meeting have different ideas. So, the same collective noun, *'meeting'* takes a plural verb – *'are'*)

More such examples are:
   a   A flock of sheep was considered a sign of prosperity.
   b. It was sad that a flock of sheep were wandering into the jungle.
   c. The crew is made up of experienced sailors.
   d. The crew were attacked by pirates at intervals.

5. Times turn bad.
6. The pain at the death is too much for them.
   These are interesting cases of Countable/Uncountable nouns. 'Time' primarily is uncountable; but 'times' in the sense 'conditions of life' is a countable plural. So, it takes the plural verb, *'turn'*. 'Pain', being abstract, is an uncountable and so is singular. Hence, *'is'*. The same thing happens in the examples below: *'Sport'*, being abstract, is singular. So is *'flattery.'*
7. But their sport disturbs and even kills many of the hares.
8. Jeet's flattery pleases Four Tusks.

In a nutshell

- 3rd person, singular subject – singular verb in present tense
- 's'-ending in the main verb makes it singular.
- Collective nouns → sing. verb, if taken as a single body
  → plu. verb, if taken individually
- Abstract nouns are uncountable
- Uncountables take singular verbs

Choose the right verbs from brackets: A team of archery players –1-(are/is) welcomed by our Principal. The team –2—(is/are) requested to sit in the chairs provided. The high spirits on their faces –3—(show/shows) their enthusiasm. These players in the team –4—(has/have) come from the neighbouring school.

Our Principal, an archery fan herself like some of us, --5—(has/have) invited them for a friendly match with our school team. Her warmth in welcoming the guest team –6—(reflects/reflect) her interest. A band of our girls –7—(has/have) practised some dances, which they will perform during the match.

In fact, the news of the archery match—8—(excite/excites)us. Such an occasion –9—(provide/provides) chances for us to meet new friends, who –10-(remain/remains) friends for long.

1.2 CONCORD – 2

{Answer to the previous questions: 1. is 2. are 3. shows 4. have 5. has 6. reflects 7. has 8. excites 9. provides 10. remain }

Please recall the story of the clever hare.

Some more examples from the story:

9. Gymnastics is alright.
10. 'Either Four Tusks or I win, not both.'
11. Every hare applauds Jeet's bravery.
12. The means Jeet has used to chase away the herd is clever, they say.

Some nouns, which look like plurals, have singular meaning and so they take only singular verbs, as in Eg. 8 above. Some other examples are:

i   Physics is related to Mathematics.
ii.   Ethics is a serious study of moral behaviour.
iii. These days, measles is well under control.
iv. No news is good news.
v.   The summons from the court was received late.

In sentence 9, the connective, *'either . . . or'* (for that matter, *'neither . . . nor'* and *'not only . . . but also'*) takes the principle of proximity and so the verb agrees with the subject nearest to it. Hence *'win'*. It is not *'wins'* to agree with the singular *'Four Tusks'* but with the nearest *'I'*, which is first person, though singular. The practice is to use *'s-ending'* with third person, singular nouns.

Some more examples are:
1. Either David or his friends make breakfast.
2. Neither honest thoughts nor a sincere word is rewarded today.
3. Not only the school captain but also all the House captains meet the Principal.

In sentence 10, *'Every'* makes the verb singular – *'applauds'*. Likewise, *'each'* and *'none'* also take singular verbs. Examples:
1. Each answer gets two marks.
2. Each of the players is awarded a prize.
3. None knows the answer.
4. None among the students volunteers to do the work.

In sentence 11, *'means'* refers to the 'method or way'. Thus, it is singular. But when the meaning of *'means'* is 'income', 'resources of wealth', it is plural. To illustrate:

The means justifies the end   (= the way/path).

There is no means to locate the lost horse (= way)

My means are too weak to support you. (= sources of income)

The firm's means stabilize it even in a potential crisis. (money sources)

There can be some confusion on the number of the verb because the number of the subject and that of the subject-complement differ. This can be solved by sticking only to the number of the subject. For example:

1a. These dictionaries were our only source of information.
1b. Our only source of information was these dictionaries.
2a. The busiest part of the day was the first two office hours.
2b. The first two office hours were the busiest part of the day.
3a. My only comfort amidst all these problems is that I'm an optimist.
3b. My only comfort amidst all these problems is the two years left in service.
4. The two years left in service are my only comfort.
5. That lady is all ears wherever she goes.

However, in sentences starting with *'What'*, the verb agrees with the complement:
5. What we need most now are 800 committed soldiers. (complement agreement)
6. What is needed most now are 800 committed soldiers. (complement agreement)

In a nutshell

- Some nouns look like plural but are in fact singular(Physics, Summons etc.)
- Verbs take the Rsmber of the nearest noun in 'Either…or', 'Neither…nor' and 'Not only…but also'
- 'Every', 'Each' and 'None' take singular verbs.
- Nouns like 'means' take sing./plu. verb, according the meaning.
- The verb should agree with the subject not with its complement.

Choose the right verbs from brackets: I know that politics—1—(are/is) good if practised in good will. When politics and good will—2—(go/goes)together, we get good statesmen. Not only politicians but also the good citizen—3—(make/makes) a prosperous country. Every citizen of the nation—4—(count/counts) a lot in the running of the country.

Each Bhutanese—5—(feel/feels) proud of the long thirty five years of the fourth King's reign. The proudest period in Bhutan History—6—(was/were) those thirty five years. Now, Bhutan is a democracy. The philosophy of the switch-over to democracy—7—(was/were) a wise conception of His Majesty's.

An educated citizenry—8—(form/forms) the backbone of any democracy. Therefore, not only Political Science but also Economics—9—(find/finds) a place in College curricula. Let education expand its horizons so that none—10—(is/are) left uneducated.

1.3 CONCORD—3

{Answer to the previous questions: 1. is 2. go 3. makes 4.counts 5. feels 6. was 7. was 8. forms 9. finds 10. is }

Read the story:

An atheist barber was trimming the beard of a believer. Throughout his work, he had a good argument with the believer regarding the existence of God. The barber gradually grew more talkative as he thought, '*He dare not talk much for fear of my mis-trimming his beard.*' The believer too thought, '*A customer like me should talk less. If I were the barber, perhaps I'd babble like him. Noble are the fruits of patience, after all.*'

After his service, the barber concluded, "*Dear friend, we each have the right to our own beliefs. But look, a lot of people are atheists today—in fact, more than are popularly thought of. For, a lot of your theism is unscientific.*"

After paying the barber, the believer was about to go. But, stopping him on his way, the barber continued passionately, "*If your God underlined existed, would there be so many poor and wretched struggling on in their lives? You claim your God is love. In fact, the poor remain poor but the rich grow richer. Is this your God's love? Look at me. I who am poor work round the clock to keep my big family alive.*"

The believer at last said, "*My dear, there is lots to talk. But I have just five minutes left to catch the bus. Five minutes is too less to convince you about God's existence.*"

By then, a shabby, unkempt, bearded beggar approached them for some money. Grabbing that chance, the believer said, *"Now I believe that barbers don't exist."* Confused and unable to control his laughter, the barber exclaimed, *"Why?"*

"The unkempt, bearded beggar means the non-existence of barbers."

"Unless he comes to me, how can I . . . ?" the barber stopped.

"Dear friend, unless we go to God, (for that matter, unless the poor go to God,) we won't know Him. Just as two and two makes four, man and God make love."

*   *   *   *   *

A study of the story above (notice the words underlined) for subject-verb agreement teaches us the following lessons:

No	Sentences	S – V agreement
1.	He <u>had</u> a good argument. The barber gradually <u>grew</u> more talk-ative.	The past tense does not follow S—V agreement (except *was* and *were*).
2.	He <u>dare</u> not talk much.	Semi-modals like *need* and *dare* in the negative do not follow S—V agreement. (But, *He dares (to) talk to her.*)
3.	A customer like me <u>should</u> talk less.	Modals do not follow S—V agreement.
4.	If I <u>were</u> the barber, . . . *If your God <u>existed</u>, . . .*	Rejected and imaginary conditionals do not follow S—V agreement.
5.	Noble <u>are</u> the fruits of patience.	In sentences of adj. or adv. beginning, the verb agrees with the actual, post-verbial subject. (*fruits*) *Sweet are the uses of adversity. *Here are the puppies of your choice.
6.	We <u>each have</u> the right.	Though *each* is singular, *we each* and *they each* are plural. Hence *have*.
7.	A lot of people <u>are</u> atheists today. A lot of your theism <u>is</u> unscientific. There <u>is</u> lots to talk.	* The singular-plural of the phrases of in-definite number such as *a lot of, some of* and *a number of etc.* is decided by the actu-al subject that follows them. are – atheists is—theism (Uncountable – sing.) * '*lots*' is plural. But '*lots*' is singular in '*lots + to – infinitive*'
8.	. . . more (atheists) than <u>are</u> popularly thought of	'*More + pl + than . . .* ' takes pl. verb, whereas '*More than one*' takes a singular noun and singular verb. *More than one computer <u>was</u> used.
9.	The poor <u>remain</u> poor but the rich <u>grow</u> richer.	Often, '*the + adj*' = *plural noun*

10.	I who <u>am</u> poor work round the clock	The verb after **relative pronouns** agrees with its antecedent. (*'Am'* agrees with its antecedent, *'I'* before the relative pronoun, *'who'*)
11.	Five minutes <u>is</u> too less to convince you.	Measurements of time, money, distance, and weight etc. take singular verbs.
12.	Two and two <u>makes</u> four.	Numerals joined with *and* or *plus* are considered singular. But, *Three and seven <u>are</u> prime numbers.*

In a nutshell

- 'A lot of', 'Some of' etc. take verbs according to the subjects that come later.
- 'The + Adjective' behaves like the plural noun.
- The verbs after the relative pronouns should agree with their antecedents.
- Plural quantity-nouns take singular verbs.

Choose the right verbs from brackets: 1. Five litres—(is/are) enough for your scooter. 2. The rich often—(avoid) walking short distances. 3. More participants than expected—(take/takes) part in the contest this time. 4. There—(is/are) lots to do. 5. It is you who—(is/are) responsible for this crime. 6. She—(need/needs) not advise you. 7. A lot of apples (is/are) rotten. 8. A lot of water—(has/have) been wasted. 9. Our decision is that they each—(tell/tells) a story. 10. You should prove that seven plus eight —(make/makes) fifteen. 11. My dear, don't you know the old saying, 'Mysterious —(is/are) the ways of God'? 12. If I —(am/were) a mosquito, I would bite my enemies.

1.4 CONCORD—4

{Answer to the previous questions: 1. is 2. avoid 3. take 4.is 5. are 6. need 7. are 8. has 9. tell 10. makes 11. are 12. were }

Read the story:
Once upon a time, there was a beautiful and gentle woman. She had no children and many a time, she wished to have a child of her own. She pitied herself, *"Even sheep and deer have their own little ones. Why not I, though a human being? This news is bad and people hate me. The gentry of the town avoid my company. I'm tired and cares weigh heavily on me."*

Then, one day, she met the left handed fairy. The latter was kind and without airs, unlike most of her kind. The fairy always held her wand in her left hand. The left handed fairy gave the woman a handful of magic seeds with this piece of advice, *"Sow them in your garden; instruct your maid-servants to guard them; see that cattle don't trample on them. Be patient. You know that slow and steady wins the race."*

The woman hurried home and scattered the seeds in her garden. She waited, slow and steady. And then, a beautiful red flower sprang out of the earth and grew up tall and straight. The woman raised her spectacles to see closer the spectacle – the red flower. She leant forward and gently kissed the flower. Soon, the petals opened and there stood inside, the prettiest little girl she had ever seen – apparently a rare human species indeed. The woman laughed and exclaimed. *"Her hair is golden and her skin is pink. But, she is no bigger than half my thumb. I shall call her Thumbelina."*

*   *   *   *   *

The language structures used in the story above tell us a few things about concord i.e. subject-verb agreement:

1. Many a/ Many an = Many. The articles 'a' or 'an' makes the noun singular.
Eg:

1. Many a time, she wished to have a child of her own. (not 'many a times, . . .)
2. Many an agreement was signed between the two countries. (not 'many an agreements were . . . ')
3. Full many a flower is born to blush unseen. (not 'many a flowers are born . . . ')
4. Many an elephant has destroyed the crops. (not 'many an elephants have . . .)
5.

2. Nouns such as 'sheep', 'deer', 'swine', 'cod', 'trout', 'species', 'series', 'works' and 'headquarters' etc. are both singular and plural, unchanged in form.
Eg:

1. The one lost sheep was brought back.—A few sheep stray into the forest.
2. The lion chases one of the deer .—Three deer in the group were quite tame.
3. The swine is considered filthy.—The butcher separated two fat swine.
4. The cod forms a delicacy on the table.—They managed to fish a dozen cod.
5. A trout costs less than a salmon does.—Some trout were killed in the oil spill.
6. We came across a new species of flies—Two species of mosquitoes are harmful.
7. A single series of cells is enough.—The warden held three series of enquiries.
8. The brick works has been in crisis—The coal works have gone for a pay hike.
9. The headquarters is very strong .—The headquarters take careful decisions.

3. Collective nouns like 'gentry', 'police', 'people', 'cattle', 'poultry' and 'vermin' take plural verbs.
Eg:

    a. The gentry in the area look down upon the peasants.
    b. The police are after the absconders.
    c. The people of Bhutan are a fun-loving sort. (Compare: *The Olympians represent the various peoples of the world.*)
    d. How long have the cattle been straying into the paddy field?
    e. She takes extra care for these poultry of hers.
    f. Rats spoil a lot of our crops; the vermin really play havoc in the field.

4. Differentiated plural. The following table shows that uncountable nouns (which do not form plurals normally) take a different meaning, when they appear as plurals:

1. The **care** he takes <u>is</u> great indeed. (care = tender feeling)	1. . . . and <u>**cares**</u> <u>weigh</u> down me.(story) (cares = anxiety)
2. This rod is made of **iron**. (iron = material)	2. Being in **irons**, the thief could not run. (irons = chains)
3. Drinking does not do you **good**. (good= benefit)	3. The **goods** in this truck <u>belong</u> to me. (goods= things)
4. The room is pleasant with fresh **air**.	4. The latter was kind and without **airs**, unlike most of her kind. (story) (airs = vanity)
5. The wound give me **pain**.	5. Alison really took **pains** to become ready for the relay race. (pains = effort)
6. I like her athletic spirit. She's always fair in **play**.	6. Shakespeare's **plays** <u>are</u> popular. (plays=dWilliamas)
7. The chair made a sensible **talk**.	7. We can solve the problem through **talks**. (talks = formal discussions)
8. **People** make laws and so laws are for them.	8. **Peoples** of India and Bhutan keep a cordial relationship. (peoples = societies)
9. The woman raised her <u>spectacles</u> to see closer the **<u>spectacle.</u>** (story) (spectacle = sight)	9. The woman raised her <u>**spectacles**</u> to see closer the <u>spectacle</u> (spectacles = eye-glasses)
10. Teachers advise us to show **respect** to our elders. (respect= high regard)	10. We shall pay our humble **respects** to the new boss (respects = compliments)
11. You need some **force** to open the box.	11. The UN **forces** went there as a peace-keeping unit. (forces = troops)
12. My father gave me good **advice**. (advice = counsel)	12. I got enough credit **advices** from the bank. (advices = information)
13.The footballer made a good **return**.(return=coming/ giving back)	13. Please show your income tax **returns**. (returns = statistics)
14. The **time** has come for us to act.	14. Hard **times** have struck his firm. (times = conditions)
15. Early snow caused **damage** to the crops.	15. The newspaper paid enough **damages** to the minister for false charges. (damages=compensation)

5. Uncountable nouns, as shown below, don't make plurals. However, they have countable equivalents, which can take plural forms.

Uncountables	Countable equivalents
1. Advice	1. **A piece of advice** from my mother helped me a lot. (not 'an advice from my mother . . .)
2. news	2. I re-read those two **items of news/ news stories**. (not 'two newses')
3.laughter	3. My grandpa had a good **laugh** at my story. (not 'a good laughter')
4. poetry	4. There are seven **poems** in the syllabus. (not 'seven poetries')
5. scenery	5. The tourists were impressed by the variety of **scenes** in the country. (not 'sceneries')
6. progress	6. Ruth made good progress(not 'a good progress')/ Ruth made a good **advance**.
7. machinery	The **machines** used here are imported ones. (not 'machinereis')
8.luggage	Will all these **pieces of luggage** go in? (not 'luggages')
9. money	Keep a few **coins/ ngultrums/ rupees** in your purse.(not 'moneys')
10. time	Three hours are pretty long . (not 'three times')

11. furniture	These **articles/pieces of furniture** look so nice to me.
12. bedding	The boys use these three **beds** as their study tables too. (not 'beddings')
13. information	Where did you get this **piece of information** from? (not 'informations')
14. employment	A few **jobs** are available in the company. (not 'employments')
15. fun	We burst out laughing at the series of **jokes** from the comedian (not 'funs')
16. luck	It was just **a stroke of luck** that he passed the exam. (not 'a luck')
17. fortune	**A stroke of fortune** alone can save from danger. (not 'a fortune')
18. bread	**A loaf of bread** is better than no bread. (not 'a bread')
19. music	It was wonderful music (not 'a wonderful music')/ It was a wonderful **song/tune**.
20. applause	Two **rounds of applause** echoed in the hall after the song. (not 'applauses')

In a Nutshell
- Say 'many a time', not 'many a times.'
- 'sheep', 'deer', 'species', 'series' and 'works' etc. are both singular and plural
- 'police', 'cattle' and 'poultry' etc. are always plural.
- care/cares, advice/advices and people/peoples etc. have different meanings.
- advice, furniture and luggage etc. can have countable equivalents.

Don't say	Say
1. a news	*1. a news-item*
2. a poetry/poetries	*2. a poem*
3. a fun	*3. a joke*
4. a luggage / luggages	*4. a piece of luggage*
5. an advice /advices	*5. a piece/ pieces of advice.*

Now, try these:
- It was a fine -------(music / song)
- It was fine ---------(music / song)
- Did you lose all your-----(luggage / luggages) on the way?
- The Daffodils is a good ---- (poetry / poem)
- The Daffodils is good----(poetry/ poem)
- My neighbour complained that my cattle --- (was/were) destroying his paddy.
- --- (Care/Cares) often make people look tired.
- The bombing caused a great deal of --- (damage/damages) to the town.
- Both the species --- (are/ is) protected plants.
- Many a deer ---- (has/ have) been killed in the drought.
- The tourist guide took great --- (pain/pains) to help the tourists.
- She is struggling to get a government ---- (job/ employment).
- A --- (laugh/ laughter) by one can make others laugh.
- What a marvellous ---- (scene/scenery)!
- The audience sat silent, listening to fine --- (music/ tune)

{Answer to the previous questions : 1.song 2. music 3. luggage 4. poem 5. poetry
6.were 7. Cares 8. damage 9. are 10. has 11. pains 12. job 13. laugh 14.scene 15. music}

2. ARTICLES

Read the story and notice the use of articles (shown with Rsmbers):

"Be a (1) Roman when you are in (2) Rome," said(3) Grandpa while shaking hands with me on my departure on a (4)European tour. Though I did not speak all the European languages, I thought I would manage with (5)English.

My air flight, which was across the (6) Himalayas, was enjoyable. I must have crossed the (6 a) Ganges and the Brahmaputra too. The flight had a short halt in London, which is in the (7) UK, before it proceeded to Paris. Before the flight reached London, I had had (8) breakfast and, owing to (9) diabetes, sugarless tea in the flight. As we landed in London, (10) the sun was concealed by the clouds in the sky and it was dark and gloomy around. An honourable man next to me asked me in (11) earnest, "Isn't it too long (12) a journey for a (13) young man like you?"

1. : 'a' before a countable singular noun, '*Roman*', with a consonant beginning.
2. : zero article (no article) before a proper noun, '*Rome*'.
3. : zero article before nouns of family relations.
4. : 'a' before a countable singular noun, with a consonant sound ('y')(also in 13)
5. : zero article before names of languages.
6. : 'the' is used before the names of mountain ranges and rivers (6 a) and oceans.
7. : 'the' is used before the names of nations, indicating 'a union of . . . '
8. : zero article before nouns of meals.
9. : zero article before nouns of diseases.
10. : 'the' is used before things which are unique.
11. : zero article in common phrases (don't say 'in an earnest' or 'in the earnest').
12. : after 'so' or 'too' + adj/adv , use an article.

Study the following table and take care of the use, misuse and non-use of the articles:

Examples	Guidelines to the use	Error
1. a. In Austria, people speak German. 1 b. Can you speak French? 1 c. The French are fashionable people.	*no articles before the names of languages. * 'the English'/ the German(s) = the people of England/ the citizen/people of Germany. The French = the people of France	1. a. <u>The</u> English is a world language. 1 b. Can you speak <u>the</u> French? 1 c. French are fashionable people.
2. Man does not live by bread alone.	* 'The' is not used before 'man' or 'woman', when they are in general sense.	2. <u>The</u> man does not live by bread alone.
3. She thanked me for the present I gave her. **Compare:** 4. <u>Gold</u> is found in Australia and South Africa. 5. <u>The Gold</u> found in Australia is of pure quality.	* 'The' is used to refer to particular things. Here, 'present I gave her' makes the 'present' particular. * 'Gold' in 5 is 'gold' in general – like all material nouns (iron, copper and glass etc.) it takes zero article – no article. 'Gold' in 6 is made particular by 'found in Aus . . . '	3. She thanked me for present I gave her. 4. The Gold is found in Australia and South Africa. 5. Gold found in Australia is of pure quality.
6. Selfishness is an evil quality.	* 'Selfishness', being an abstract noun (like 'beauty', 'truth', 'wisdom' and 'cruelty' etc.), takes zero article.	6. The selfishness is an evil quality.
7. The *Pacific Ocean* is calmer than the *Atlantic Ocean*.	* 'The' is used before the names of rivers, oceans, seas, lakes, gulfs, mountain ranges and groups of islands etc. Eg: 'The Ganges', 'The Atlantic ocean', 'The Persian Gulf', 'The Himalayas', 'The Maldives'. But, 'Malta lies in the central Mediterranean sea.' (Names of individual islands take zero article.)	7. a. *Pacific Ocean* is calmer than *Atlantic Ocean*. 7. b. Crossing Persian gulf is fairly easy. 7. c. Adventurous people inhabit British Isles. 7. d. The calm waters of Pacific Ocean run deep.

8.a. Mount Everest is the highest peak. 8.b. Kanchenjunga is in Nepal.	*Names of mountain peaks take zero article.	8. a. The Mount Everest is the highest peak. 8. b. The Kanchenjunga is in Nepal.
9. a. A live ass is better than a dead lion. 9. b. <u>A</u> bird in hand is worth two in <u>the</u> bush.	* 'ass' and 'lion' are countable singular and represent all asses and lions (the genus). Such **generic singulars** often take 'the'. Eg: *The cow is useful.* All countable singulars take an article.	9. a. Live ass is better than dead lion. 9. b. Bird in hand is worth two in bush 9. c. Lion is a dangerous animal. 9. d. Teacher draws picture on the board.
10. a. Brutus is an honourable man. 10. b. . An honour was conferred on my uncle. An 10. c. That was not a very honest thing to do. 10. d. My opinion was accepted by a unanimous vote. 10.e. All respect an honest man. 10. f. We can achieve it only through a united effort. 10. g. This is a university progWilliamme. 10. h. Such an extra lesson was necessary. 10. i. We haven't solved so complex a problem. 10 j. I have a little time to spare. 10. k. We have a few boys to help us.	* 'an' is used before all vowel sounds, irrespective of the alphabet that begins the word. In spite of the 'h-beginning', 'honourable' starts with an 'o' sound. Hence 'an honourable'. But 'a united', 'a university', 'a year', 'a young man', 'a European', 'a one-eyed man' and so on. *Use 'a' or 'an' after 'such' if the noun that follows is a countable singular. ('*lesson*') * 'a'/ 'an' is used between the noun (*problem*) and the adjective (*complex)* ('so'+ adj) 'A little' = some 'Little' = practically nothing 'A few' = some 'Few' = practically not many	10. a. Brutus is a honourable man. 10. b. A honour was conferred on my uncle. 10. c..That was not very honest thing to do. 10. d. My opinion was accepted by an unanimous vote. 10. e. All respect a honest man. 10. f. We can achieve it only through an united effort. 10. g. This is an university progWilliamme. 10.h. Such extra lesson was necessary. 10.i. We haven't solved a so complex problem. 10.j. I have little time to spare. (=I can't wait) 10. k. We have few boys to help us.(= they're of no use)

11. <u>The</u> Queen takes keen interest in the people's welfare.	* 'The' is used before 'King', 'Queen' 'President' and Principal' etc. when not followed by their names. So, we say: 'The President visits us.' But, 'President Obama visits us.' 'The King is concerned . . . ' But, 'King Hussein is concerned . . . ' etc. *(However, we must say: 'She was <u>elected President</u> unanimously'. 'Michael <u>became Principal</u> in 1990.')*	11. a. The Queen Victoria encouraged art. 11. b. The President Salim Khan ordered an inquiry.
12. <u>The</u> *Queen Elizabeth* is a notable British ship.	* 'The' is used before: i. names of ships/trains ii. do of musical instruments iii. superlatives (except : *'like most/best'; 'a most rewarding career'*)	12. *Mayflower* took the settlers from Plymouth to America.
13. Alison is good at <u>the</u> guitar.		13. Alison is good at guitar.
14. I have got <u>the</u> most convincing evidence. *Exception:* 'Which mode of learning do you <u>like best</u>?' 'His was <u>a most</u> interesting narration.'		14. I have got most convincing evidence. *Exception:* 'Which mode of learning do you like the best?' 'His was <u>the most</u> interesting narration.' ('the most interesting = the superlative; a most interesting = very interesting.)
15. i. <u>The</u> sun is the source of all energy. i. <u>The</u> *'Iliad'* is an epic. ii. I saw it in <u>the</u> *'Herald'* iii. <u>The</u> USA stands greater than <u>the</u> Netherlands. iv. The car hit her on the knee.	* 'The' is used before names of: i. things unique ii. great works/ holy books. iii. newspapers/ magazines iv. countries suggesting groups of smaller units.(the UK . . .) v. *do* of parts of the body or of the dress.	15. i. Sun is the source of all energy. i. *'Iliad'* is an epic. ii. I saw it in *'Herald'* iii.USA stands greater than Netherlands. iv. The car hit her on knee.
ii. i. I have had long years of dealings with <u>the</u> Grand Bank. ii. <u>The</u> Central Library has been doing good down the years.	'The' is used before names of Departments, Corporations and Govt. units etc. 'Columbia University' but 'the University of Columbia', 'the RUB' etc.	16. i. School of Pedagogy is customer-friendly in its work. University of Cambridge has been popular. iii. Having been from the Oxford University, she talks substance.

17.i. Every day we go to church to attend the Holy Mass. ii. Yesterday, I went to the school to meet my son.	'The' is not used if we go *there* for the usual purpose (for example, 'church to pray' and 'school to study' etc.). If not, avoid 'the'.	i. In order to study the architecture there, I went to church. (the church) ii. My daughter goes to the school daily except on Sundays. (to school)
18. i. I have a pink and an orange shirt ii. The teacher and singer taught us grammar.	* The articles 'a' and 'an' are separately used here, meaning there are two shirts. If there is only one shirt with pink and orange patterns, then we say, 'I have a pink and orange shirt.' *Likewise, the sentence, 18 ii., refers to just one person because there is only one article ('the').	
19. i. I go home at 7.00	*Nouns in set phrases like 'strike root', 'face to face', 'set fire', 'in debt' etc. take no articles. (*Note: 'home'* and *'abroad'* on the left are adverbs)	19. i. The parcel came by the post.
ii. She is working abroad.		ii. It happened at the night.
iii. The plant strikes root.		iii. He rang me up by a mistake.

Exercise: 1. a. Supply 'a'/ 'an'/ 'the'/ zero article in the following sentences:

1. —(king) is an immensely respected figure in Bhutan.
2. —(man) is a social animal.
3. Of all the women I have known, my mother is definitely—(best).
4. History tells us that we have fought many wars against—(Tibetans).
5. But—(English) proved especially difficult to defeat.
6. I took a basic language course in—(French).
7. This is a wonderful version of the poem translated from—(French).
8. He was badly injured in—(leg).
9. They have just returned from a holiday in—(Bahaman Islands).
10. —(one-eyed) man is a sad sight.
11. —(gold) I am talking about is 100% pure.
12. My cousin who is in Austria speaks—(German).
13. Jesus tells us that—(man) does not live by bread alone.
14. In recognition to his great work,—(honour) will be conferred on him.
15. —(unanimous) vote is required for the passing of the bill.
16. We stand strong because of—(united) exercise.
17. —(honest) person is held in high esteem.
18. I am proud of—(sacrifice) our soldiers made.
19. All want—(experienced) coach.
20. —(polar bear) is a gentle animal.
21. Marconi is believed to be the inventor of—(radio)
22. Charles Dickens poularised—(genre) called, 'novel'.
23. —(young) girl of good looks can be a promise in the film world.

24. I would like to drive—(home) the message of patriotism.
25. —(Prime Minister) gives the keynote address.

1. b. *Supply the articles a, an, the in or remove them from the following sentences where necessary:*

1. Have you ever seen so tall man?
2. It was such absurd story.
3. You will never see so large house.
4. He hopes to become teacher in future.
5. We have had very tiring journey.
6. To go to heaven as one-eyed man is better than to go to heaven with two sinning eyes, says Bible.
7. Not only English but also all Christians globally believe in it.
8. Even Brutus, honourable man, acted accordingly.
9. Hospital you were referring to is near City Bank
10. Extravagant youth leads to sorrowful age.
11. The impudence can ruin one's future.
12. My uncle gave good decision.
13. The *Ganges* is muddier than *Brahmaputra*.
14. The Mount Etna has a volcano.
15. The waters of Indian Ocean go rough.
16. Bird in hand is better than two in bush.
17. Hard working man is honourable man.
18. Early bird catches worm.
19. Man is curious and hard working.
20. German are industrious people.
21. Ink is useful thing.
22. *Ivanhoe* is historical novel.
23. The jealousy is an evil passion.
24. I saw dog coming towards me.
25. The *MD* is overall coordinator.
26. The Mount *Ghangkar Phuensum* is the highest unclimbed peak in the world.
27. Bay of Bengal separates India from Myanmar.
28. Dead man tells no tales.
29. It was unique sight.
30. Khan I like most is Kader Khan.

Answers: 1. a.

1. The 2. zero article 3.the 4. the 5. the 6. zero article 7. zero article 8. the 9. the 10. A 11. The 12. zero article 13. zero article 14. an 15. A 16. a 17. An 18. the 19. an 20. The 21. the 22. the 23. A 24. zero article 25. The

1. b.
1. Have you ever seen so tall a man?
2. It was such an absurd story.

3. You will never see so large a house.

4. He hopes to become a teacher in future.

5. We have had a very tiring journey.

6. To go to heaven as a one-eyed man is better than to go to heaven with two sinning eyes, says Bible.

7. Not only the English but also all Christians globally believe in it.

8. Even Brutus, an honourable man, acted accordingly.

9. The hospital you were referring to is near BOD

10. Extravagant youth leads to sorrowful age.

11. Impudence can ruin one's future.

12. My uncle gave a good decision.

13. The *Ganges* is muddier than the *Brahmaputra*.

14. Mount Etna has a volcano.

15. The waters of the Indian Ocean go rough.

16. A bird in the hand is better than two in the bush.

17. A hard working man is an honourable man.

18. An early bird catches the worm.

19. Man is curious and hard working.

20. The German are an industrious people.

21. Ink is a useful thing.

22. *Ivanhoe* is a historical novel.

23. Jealousy is an evil passion.

24. I saw a dog coming towards me.

25. The *MD* is an overall coordinator.

26. Mount *Ghangkar Phuensum* is the highest unclimbed peak in the world.

27. The Bay of Bengal separates India from Myanmar.

28. A/ The dead man tells no tales.

29. It was a unique sight.

30. The Khan I like most is Kader Khan.

3. A GLANCE AT TENSES IN ENGLISH

Read the story below:

Once there lived two frogs—David and Martin. They were very good friends – they walked, joked and ate together. The proverb says, "A friend in need is a friend indeed." So, they were available in each other's needs.

One day, they <u>were walking</u> together, telling each other stories of old. David, being careless, <u>did not see</u> a tank of milk just in front of him. Martin saw the tank and was about to warn him. But David <u>had fallen</u> into it before Martin <u>warned</u> him. "Help, help," screamed David from the tank. "My God! My friend <u>will drink</u> a lot of milk. But, too much of anything is bad," Martin thought.

Martin stretched his hands down to David in order to pull him out. But, in the attempt, he too slipped into the tank.

Now see, both friends <u>leap</u> and <u>leap</u>. And leap . . .
The milk <u>gets</u> splashed, splashed. And splashed . . .

But, all was in vain. David, being very tired, a last gave up, "Dear," David said, " I'm dying. I <u>have lost</u> all my energy. I can no longer jump. By the time you get out from the tank, <u>I'll have been</u> a dead frog. I am sure . . . sure . . . that you <u>will offer</u> some butter lamps for me when you visit a monastery next, you will offer some butter lamps for me when you visit a monastery next. Bye . . . all the luck."

But, Martin went on jumping. As he <u>was jumping</u>, he felt something solid on his feet. He climbed onto it and jumped. Hurray!!! Up came Martin out of the tank.

He had peeped into the pond before he <u>proceeded</u> to the monastery. Down there, he had seen some solid object – was it his friend's dead body or butter??

The above story shows the common uses of the commonly used tenses in English. Let's consider them one by one.

1. **Simple present**
The examples in the story are:
    1. *The proverb says . . .*

2. *A friend in need is a friend indeed.*

These examples show permanent truths (*A friend in need is*). Besides, we use simple present to quote old sayings.(*says*). We also use the simple present for habitual actions in the present such as:

My father gets up at 4.00 every morning.

The example given below tells us about the use of the Historic present/ DWilliamatic present. Interestingly, the writer has suddenly moved from past tense to the simple present in the middle of the story.

- *Now see, both friends leap and leap. And leap . . .*
- *The milk gets splashed, splashed. And splashed . . .*

Writers use the Historic present for clarity and immediacy, as if the incidents were taking place just now in front of our eyes.

.

We use simple present to write reviews, appreciations, commentaries of books, films and such artistic works.

  Elizabeth Jennings uses the first person point of view in *The Cabbage White Butterfly*
  The *Tom and Jerry* serials give human abilities to animals.

2. Present continuous/ progressive

The example from the story'

. . . they were walking together
shows an action in contiRsity or progression – 'be +—ing'

The following example has an action in the near future definitely planned:

  The PM is visiting us tomorrow. (The PM visits us . . . is also possible)
  She is buying a new car next week.

(Note: Likewise, though both *We are playing the match tomorrow* and *We play the match tomorrow* are acceptable, only the passive progressive—*The match is being played tomorrow*—is acceptable, not *The match is played tomorrow*)

To talk emphatically about some action, we sometimes use the present progressive form:

He is always disturbing me, Sir.
The kids are frequently misplacing my books, Mom.

The following are some of the **verbs of state, perception and cognition**. Normally, they are **not used** in the 'be +—ing' form—be it present continuous or past continuous.

> see, hear, smell, touch, feel, know, have, love, wish, believe, recognize, remember, forget, mean, want, seem, (dis)like, contain etc. especially followed by a *'that-clause'*

Correct	Incorrect	Could mean
1. I see the plane/ I can see…	I am seeing the plane	I have hallucinations of…
2. I hear my goat bleating	I am hearing …	I'm hearing well after medication.
3. I smell something burning	I am smelling…	I'm smelling at the pot (sniffing)
4. I feel better today	I am feeling…	I'm feeling better today (temporary)
5. I have two brothers	I am having …	I'm having nice time with my friends(enjoying)

1. a. They <u>stage</u> the cultural show tomorrow.	Fixed already and is formal
b. They're <u>staging</u> the cultural show tomorrow.	A present plan and is informal
2.a. We <u>visit</u> you all next Thursday	Not normally used
b. We <u>are visiting</u> you all next Thursday	Normally used and is fairly informal
3. a. The college <u>faces</u> the river.	Not normally used
b. The college <u>is facing</u> the river	Normally used. Though 'face' is a *stative verb*, 'facing' here is a predicative adjective more than a verb

3. **Present perfect** (to be discussed in detail in the next chapter)

4. **Simple past**
The examples from the story,

> David, being careless, did not see a tank of milk.
> . . . they walked, joked and ate together.
> Martin saw the tank and was about to warn him.

The verbs underlined talk about actions in the past and they are the second form of the verb.

First form (infinitive)	Second form	Third form (past participle)
does/do not see	did not see	had not seen
walk	walked	walked
joke	joked	joked
warn	warned	warned
is (be)	was	been

Other examples: eat	ate	eaten
see	saw	seen

The verbs that take '-ed' (1, 2 and 3 above for example) are **regular verbs** and others are **irregular verbs**.

A few more irregular verbs are given below:

First form (infinitive)	Second form	Third form (past participle)
arise	arose	arisen
awake	awoke	awaked/ awakened
bear	bore	born/borne
begin	began	begun
bid	bade	bidden
bind	bound	bound
break	broke	broken
bring	brought	brought
choose	chose	chosen
cling	clung	clung
creep	crept	crept
deal	dealt	dealt
draw	drew	drawn
dream	dreamed/dreamt	dreamed/dreamt
drive	drove	driven
dwell	dwelt	dwelt
fall	fell	fallen
feed	fed	fed
feel	felt	felt
flee	fled	fled
flow	flowed	flowed
fly	flew	flown
forbid	forbade	forbidden
forsake	forsook	forsaken
freeze	froze	frozen
grind	ground	ground
hang	hung/hanged (before death)	hung/hanged
hide	hid	hidden
kneel	knelt	knelt
lay	laid	laid

lie (in a bed)	lay	lain
lie (tell a lie)	lied	lied
lean	leaned/leant	leaned/leant
learn	learned/learnt	learned/learnt
lose	lost	lost
run	ran	run
shrink	shrank	shrunk
swear	swore	sworn
tread	trod	trodden
wind	wound	wound

Some verbs are the same in all the three forms

bet - bet   - bet
burst – burst – burst
cast – cast – cast
cost -cost - cost
hurt – hurt – hurt
let   - let - let

We use simple past for habitual actions in the past. Note that we can also use *'used to'* and *'would'* for the same purpose.

We <u>offered</u> butter lamps at the monastery every day.
We <u>used to offer</u> butter lamps at the monastery every day.
We <u>would offer</u> butter lamps at the monastery every day.

5. **<u>Simple past along with past continuous/progressive</u>**

The example from the story,

As he <u>was jumping</u>, he <u>felt</u> something solid on his feet.

speaks of a continuous action (*was jumping*) and a sudden action (*felt*). Note that the sudden action is in simple past. Some more examples:

My uncle <u>came</u> when I <u>was having</u> dinner.
I <u>was speaking</u> when the light went off.
The accident <u>occurred</u> when the bus <u>was moving</u>.

6. **<u>Past Perfect</u>**

Let's look at the sentence from the story,

David **had fallen** into it before Martin **warned** him.

The sentence talks of two past actions – *fall* and *warn*. Of these, *fall* takes place first, i.e. *before Martin warned him*. So, **the first or the earlier action** is in the past perfect – *had fallen(i.e. 'had + past participle')*.

One can remember the 'past perfect *mantra*': before 'before' or *after 'after'*.

Note that 'had fallen' comes before the word 'before'. And, it will come after the word 'after' if we recast the same sentence as:

Martin warned him after David had fallen into it.

* **In reported speech**, we use past perfect if the direct speech has past tense in it. For example,
He said that he had visited the museum already.
Here, the action of his *saying* takes place only after his *visit* of the museum. That is, the *visit* is the earlier action and hence *had visited*.

7. Simple future

Martin, in the story, thinks of his friend, David's drinking milk soon (future):
        My friend <u>will drink</u> a lot of milk.

Thus, simple future tense uses either *'shall'* or *'will'* along with the infinitive (the first form, as discussed earlier.)

    Shall—with first person (I, we) Eg: *I shall call you; we shall read it again.*
    Will—with second and third persons (meaning, with all except *'I'* and *'we'*)

Though this is the traditional use, in informal style, *'shall'* is often replaced by *'will'*

Formal	*Informal*
I shall wait for you at the bridge.	*I will wait for you at the bridge.*
We shall finish the work soon.	*We will finish the work soon.*
Kate will give me a lift.	*Kate will give me a lift.*
It will rain in the evening.	*It will rain in the evening.*

In formal style *'will + first person'* shows determination. So does *'shall + second and third persons'*
        I <u>will reject</u> his request, come what may.
        They <u>shall not cross</u> this gate so long as I am the gatekeeper.

* **Shall** is used along with the third person in official and legal documents:
        The examinee <u>shall enter</u> the examination hall five minutes before the start time.
        Every member in the hall <u>shall rise</u> as the Chief Guest arrives.
        He who violates the rule <u>shall be</u> deemed a rebel.
* **Shall** is used to denote present habitual activities and scientific truths.

In sadness, she <u>will spend</u> time all alone in her room.
Salt <u>will dissolve</u> readily in water.

Let's examine the sentence below, taken from the story:

. . . you <u>will offer</u> some butter lamps for me when you visit a monastery next.

Please note that the subordinate *when-clause* or *if-clause* is in **simple present** and the main clause is in **simple future**.

More examples:

I <u>shall not sleep</u>	until my dad <u>returns.</u>
We <u>shall go</u> for a walk	when the rain <u>stops.</u>
It <u>will rain</u> well	if the wind <u>blows.</u>
I <u>shall wear</u> a sweater	in case it <u>rains.</u>
Alison <u>will dance</u> well	if only you <u>sing</u> well.
I <u>will be fifty</u>	when my sister <u>is</u> forty.
He <u>is going to leave</u> the town	when his air ticket <u>is</u> ready.

Sentence 4 above can be re-written as:

> *I <u>shall wear</u> a sweater if it <u>should rain.</u>*

Here, '*should rain*' replaces '*rains*' to give the tone of an unlikely condition. (Most probably, it will not rain.)

*Will** acts as a finite verb in sentences like: *I won't regret my failure if God wills it so.*

8. **<u>Future perfect.</u>**

The sentence from the story:

> *By the time you get out from the tank, I'll have been a dead frog.*

shows that an action will be completed (*the death of the frog, David*) by a certain time in future (*by the time Martin gets out from the tank*)
Likewise,

> *She <u>will have finished</u> all her exams by the time her uncles returns from abroad.*
> *By the time you reach the hospital, the doctor <u>will have left</u>.*
> *Let's keep some packed food; all hotels <u>will have been closed</u> when we reach there.*

*Will have/Shall have + pp** interestingly can also indicate a past possibility. But the speaker does not know whether that possibility was fulfilled or not.

My nephew will have started from home. ('may have started' is also acceptable)
You will have noticed that my brother has become unusually silent.

When we add the 'continuity' element in future perfect, it becomes future perfect continuous. Eg:
When you reach there, most probably, the dancing practice will have been going on. So, you can join the practice.

In a Nutshell

- Use simple present for truths, present habits and the dramatic present.
- Verbs of state, perception and cognition are not used in *'be +—ing'*
- We use the second form of the verb in the *simple past.*
- The first action, of the two actions in the past, is expressed in *'had+ pp.'* *(before 'before' and after 'after')*
- *'Shall'* goes with 'I' and 'we', and *'Will'* goes with other nouns and pronouns and the reverse is the case when determination is conveyed.
- Official and legal statements make use of *'shall'.*

Use the correct tenses in the blanks below:

1. These days, prices _____ (shoot) up unnoticed.
2. All know that a swallow never _____ (make) spring.
3. Three tones of cotton, everyone _____ (know), _____ (weigh) the same as three tones of steel.
4. What will happen if the sun _____ (forget) to rise in the east?
5. He will apologise when good sense _____ (prevail).
6. I _____ (know) him for ten years now.
7. It _____ (rain) for half an hour now.
8. When we reached the school, the assembly _____ (start).
9. We _____ (have) our lunch when you visited us.
10. A cat came in when I _____ (teach).
11. Being in a hurry, I cut my finger yesterday and I _____ (bleed) for a while.
12. My house now has no roof. The roof _____ (blow) off by the wind.
13. By the time I reach home this afernoon, the lunch _____ (prepare).
14. It was winter and the river _____ (flow) gently.
15. He _____ (play) football rgularly since 1981. He plays today too.
16. A lot of money _____ (have/has) been wasted.
17. The dogs that _____ (survive) with the crumbs that _____ (fall) from the table _____ (be) loyal to their masters.
18. After it had rained, they _____ (resume) their journey.
19. If the blind _____ (lead) the blind, both shall fall.
20. Here _____ (come) the eldest sons.
21. Before the troops entered the city, the inhabitants _____ (flee).
22. Bad news _____ (travel) fast.

23. The poetry which _____ (be) selected _____ (have) been appreciated.
24. He hit his leg when he _____ (dig) the field.
25. The hourly news _____ (broadcast) only in the mother tongue.

{**Answers:** 1. shoot 2.makes 3. weighs 4.forgets 5. prevails 6. have known 7. has been raining 8. had started 9. had had 10. was teaching 11. bled 12. has been 13. will have been prepared 14. flowed 15. has played 16. has been 17. survive; fall; are/will be 18. resumed 19. lead 20. come 21. had fled 22. travels/ travelled 23. is selected; has 24. was digging 25. is/was broadcast.}

Choose the correct answers from the brackets:

1. By this time next month, Edward—a new computer.(buys, will buy, will have bought)
2. We—Patrick this week. (haven't met, didn't meet, hadn't met)
3. This magazine—annually. (appears, appear, is appearing)
4. Tomorrow evening, the Principal—in the farewell party. (has spoken, spoke, is speaking)
5. My son—all this evening (is playing, plays, has been playing)
6. When I stayed in Los Angelus, I—football once a fortnight. (was playing, had played, played)
7. You can catch the bus if you—now. (will start, started, start)
8. My brother—who the criminal is. (knows, has known, is knowing)
9. She—writing ten minutes ago. (finishes, finished, has finished)
10. Why trouble your mother? She—a cake. (makes, has made, is making)
11. They—him the leader last Thursday. (had chosen, choose, chose)
12. Mary—to meet her daughter's teacher. (is wanting, has wanted, wants)
13. We—grammar for seven years (are studying, studied, have been studying)
14. Edward and Simon—each other for a long time. (are knowing, know, have known)
15. The stranger thanked me for what I—(did, have done, had done)
16. The Philip brothers—a manufacturing unit in the town. (are having, has, have)
17. Unfortunately, she—(was slipping, slipped, has slipped) down when she—(climbed, climbs, was climbing) up the stairs yesterday.
18. Will the baby drink milk before it—(go, goes, will go) to bed?
19. Watch! Here—the last one of the missiles. (will go, go, goes)
20. He looked happy because he—his opponents in the debate.(beats, was beating, had beaten)

{**Answers:** 1. will have bought 2. haven't met 3. appears 4. is speaking. 5. has been playing 6.played 7. start 8. knows 9. finished 10. is making 11. chose 12. wants 13. have been studying 14. have known 15. have done 16. have 17. slipped; was climbing. 18. goes 19. goes 20. had beaten.}

Edit and rewrite the following sentences:

1. Last week I had been to Kolkata to buy some books for the school.
2. I am not talking to him so far.
3. Michael is working round the clock for the last two weeks.
4. We shall meet when the rain will stop.
5. My teacher is understanding my situation.
6. I asked them who was knowing the answer.
7. My father has heard the news yesterday itself.
8. My God! My daughter did not return from the school yet.

9. My uncle, who is having a car, can go wherever he wants to go.
10. Don't listen to her if she will insult you.
11. William is absent for a week now.
12. When have you seen the manager?
13. You look so tired because you worked hard in the office.
14. Have you visited the museum when you were in Sudan?
15. My son ate all the biscuits and now there is nothing left.
16. My sister has been working in this factory since three years.
17. Young Tom was playing computer games till his Dad returned.
18. Young Tom played computer games when his Dad returned.
19. He forgot to post the letter I gave him.
20. When the child lay in the cradle, a spider stung it.
21. She shall be discussing the matter with you.
22. He will have been finishing the project work by the end of the month.
23. I did not see her since we have had dinner together once.
24. Sheila is working for the project for the whole week. Today she takes a day off.
25. I caught him red-handed; when I was coming in, he removed the phone cables.

Answers:
1. Last week I went to Kolkata to buy some books for the school.
2. I have not talked to him so far.
3. Michael has been working /has worked round the clock for the last two weeks.
4. We shall meet when the rain stops.
5. My teacher understands my situation.
6. I asked them who knew the answer.
7. My father heard the news yesterday itself.
8. My God! My daughter has not returned from the school yet.
9. My uncle, who has a car, can go wherever he wants to go.
10. Don't listen to her if she insults you.
11. William has been absent for a week now.
12. When did you see the manager?
13. You look so tired because you have worked hard in the office.
14. Did you visit the museum when you were in Sudan?
15. My son has eaten all the biscuits and now there is nothing left.
16. My sister has been working in this factory for three years.
17. Young Tom had been playing computer games till his Dad returned.
18. Young Tom was playing computer games when his Dad returned.
19. He forgot to post the letter I had given him.
20. When the child was lying in the cradle, a spider stung it.
21. She will be discussing the matter with you.
22. He will have finished the project work by the end of the month.
23. I have not seen her since we had dinner together once.
24. Sheila has been working for the project for the whole week. Today she . . . .
25. I caught him red-handed; when I came in, he was removing the phone cables.

3.1 I HAVE KNOWN HIM FOR YEARS (PRESENT PERFECT TENSE)

Read the story:

Once a flock of doves, led by their king, flew in search of food. After a long flight, one of them said sadly, "Your Majesty, we're really tired because we have flown so long." The king, encouraged them to fly a little more and luckily, they found some rice grains under a banyan tree. While happily eating the grains, a huge net fell over them and they were trapped in it. The doves tried their best to come out but in vain.

Seeing this, the hunter was very happy but the doves were very sad seeing the fowler, approaching.

However, the king of doves did not lose heart and he advised them, "Unity is strength. Each of us should clutch the net in the beak and fly up together. Now, come on and let's fly."

The birds lifted the net and flew high. The hunter was surprised. He stood there helpless and told himself, "They are able to lift my heavy net as they have put their strength together." The doves flew high over hills and valleys.

After a while, they landed on a hill, where a mouse lived. The king dove said, "The mouse was an old friend of mine. I have known him for years. When the mouse heard the loud noise of the doves' landing, he got so scared that he hid deeper into his burrow. The king dove shouted at the burrow's entrance, "Dear friend, we are in great difficulty. Please come out and help us." The mouse recognized its old friend and came out. He was so happy that he shed tears of joy. He said, "We haven't met each other for quite some time."

The king dove requested him to nibble the net and set them free. The mouse immediately started nibbling the net around the king dove. The king dove said," No, dear. First set my followers free. A king should be free after his subjects are free."

Praising the king for his nobility, the mouse nibbled at the net and, one by one, all the doves got free. The doves learned that union is strength and a friend in need is a friend indeed.

The sentences underlined in the story above have **'has/have + Past participle'**:
- . . . we have flown . . .   (have + pp of 'fly')
- . . . they have put their strength together.   (have + pp of 'put')
- I have known him for years.   (have + pp of 'know')
- We haven't met each other for quite some time."   (have + pp of 'meet')

Now, notice the pattern:

Started in the past	The effect in the present	Name of the usage
1. flying (have flown)	1. flying continues	CONTIRSATIVE USE
2. putting their strength together (have put)	2. lifting of the net	RESULTATIVE USE
3. knowing him (have known)	3. still know him.	CONTIRSATIVE USE
4. not meeting (haven't met)	4. desire to meet	Both CONT.& RESULT.

The most important feature of PRESENT PERFECT tense is that it has a reference to the <u>anteriority</u> of the past event that continues to and includes the speech time. However, the pastness is <u>indefinite</u>.

- So, definite past words such as 'yesterday', 'last week' 'an hour ago' and so on cannot be used in this tense.

- Words such as 'sometimes', 'often', 'always', 'at times', 'just', 'already', 'yet', 'ever', 'never', 'lately', 'today', 'this morning', 'this month', 'this year', 'so far', 'to date', 'over the last few weeks' and 'up to now', etc are used. Some of them are used for just completed actions – for the recency of actions (Eg: The Head Teacher has just gone; Someone has removed the statue.)

- No wonder, sentences such as 'When have you met my brother?' are unacceptable. Here, we must use *'When did you meet my brother?'* (Simple past).

To illustrate further:
- You are wet now   Have you been in the rain?
- You have runny nose   Have you had a bad cold?
- It is very cold in your room   Have you forgotten to switch on the room heater?

(a) This is called the **resultative use of the present perfect**.

Past action	The result in the present
You have been in the rain.	So, you are wet now.
You have had a bad cold.	So, you have a running nose.
You have forgotten to switch	So, your room feels very cold. on the room heater.

Study the following sentences:
- I have stayed with him since we were school mates.
- He has never loved his village.
- I have wanted to meet my brother for years.
- This bow and arrow have always belonged to my uncle.

(b) This is called the **continuative use of the present perfect**

Verbs used above—*know, love, want, belong* – show states. They are **stative verbs** and are not used in present perfect except along with frequency-words such as those used above (since, for, always etc)

Notice the use of **'since'** in No 1 and **'for'** in No 3.

Since + point of time

For + period of time

Sentence 1 above gives an interesting study:

Present perfect ('have stayed')—*'since'* + simple past ('were')

More examples:

I **have been** with the new Principal since he **came** here.

I **have been** with the new Principal <u>for</u> three years.

I **have been** in teaching since the new school **started**.

I **have been** in teaching for ten years now.

My sister **has been** here <u>since</u> life **became** normal here.

My sister has been here <u>for</u> six months.

We **haven't received** any news from him <u>since</u> we last **met**.

We **haven't received** any news from him <u>for</u> several months.

In a nutshell

- Has/ have + pp makes present perfect tense.
- The tense is used for the present result of past actions, the present contiRsation of past actions, recent events, and often used along with ever, never, just, already and yet etc.

Answer the following, using either the simple past or the present perfect tense:

1. My parents—(arrive) at Paris in 1986 and—(live) there ever since.
2. You say you—(not hear) from your brother for the past five years.
3. Last Monday we—(go) to our friends and—(stay) with them ever since.
4. My mother is not home; she—(go) to attend to a sick aunty of hers.
5. Our school captains —(go) out at 2.30 and —- (not return) yet.
6. The meeting—(discuss) the matter at length. So, we need not consider the matter again.
7. My nephews in the hostel—(have) no money since last Tuesday.
8. Your speaking skill—(grow) very much since I—(meet) you last.
9. My nieces—(not write) to us since last Christmas.
10. They—(rate) her highly as a singer since I—(hear) her last.
11. They—(not talk) to each other since they—(have)a quarrel.
12. 12.Since a baby—(bear), the parents—(be) very happy.
13. The house is clean now. Someone—(mop) the floors.
14. I—(be) to Senegal. I went there in July.
15. I—(not dine)with you since we—(eat) together during last Christmas.
16. I'd like to meet a yeti; I—(not meet) with one.
17. The Simon's—(move) in to Los Angelus in 1983; They—(be) there a long time now.

{**Answers:** 1. arrived; have lived 2. have not heard 3. went; have stayed 4. has gone 5. went; have not returned 6. has discussed 7. have had 8. has grown; met 9.have not written10. have rated; heard 11. have not talked; had 12. is/was born; have/had been 13. has mopped 14. have been 15. have not dined; ate 16. have not met 17. moved; have been}

3.2   THE COMMON CONFUSION
between present perfect and simple past IS CLEARED BELOW

(**PRESNT PERFECT** – *has/have* + *PP,* where *PP* is the 3rd form of the verb. SIMPLE PAST uses the 2nd form of the verb. Eg: *write—wrote—written*)

(1   2   3)

No.	Present Perfect	Simple Past

1.	**Continuative use:** started in the past and contiRses now, i.e. at the time of speaking. 1.a. Daniel <u>has cultivated</u> paddy here since 1978
	Daniel <u>has cultivated</u> paddy here for thirty years.
	
	1. b.Paul and Alison <u>have taught</u> Maths since 2003.
		Daniel <u>cultivated</u> paddy here in 1978. (This does not tell us whether s/he cultivated paddy after 1978 or cultivates it now or not)
		cultivate—cultivated—cultivated
		   1 2 3
		Damber and Alison <u>taught</u> Maths since 2003.
		teach—taught—taught
		   1 2 3

2.	**Resultative use:** The result of a past action is seen in the present 2. a. Harry <u>has injured</u> his/her leg. (The injury took place in the past and Harry is suffering in the present – for example, s/he is unable to play today.) 2. b. We <u>have discussed</u> the reforms of the Queen. (So, no need to discuss them now ; students already know it.) 2.c. I <u>have had</u> breakfast. (So, please don't compel me to have it now.)	2. a. Harry <u>injured</u> his/her leg. (No consideration of whether s/he can play or not.) *injure—injured—injured* 1 2 3 2. b. We <u>discussed</u> the reforms of the Queen. (*discuss-discussed-discussed*) 2. c. I <u>had</u> breakfast. *have—had—had* 1 2 3

3.	Never use definite/ clear past time markers such as 'yesterday', 'last week' and 'in April' etc. though 'since yesterday', 'since last week' and 'since April' etc. are possible. 3. a. I <u>have lost</u> my purse. (Don't add 'yesterday', for example.) 3.b. Liam <u>has built</u> a house. (Don't add 'in April', for example)	3. Definite/clear past time markers are acceptable and good. 3. a. I <u>lost</u> my purse yesterday. ***lose—lost lost*** 3. b. Liam <u>built</u> a house in April. ***build—built—built***

Answer the following questions:
1. The house is empty. The old man—(leave) the house.
2. It was last Friday that the boy—(leap) with joy when he heard about his result.
3. —he—(visit) his uncle since he returned from abroad?
4. They—(never travel) along this road since they once—(meet) a bear.
5. In 1961, my uncle—(shoot) a deer.
6. When the Police OC came, we all—(spring) to our feet.
7. Our aunt is a senior pilot; Uncle Toby—(fly) the plane for a decade now.
8. The Ganges—(flow) quietly ever since the Guru—(bless) it.
9. David, a fashionable lad,—(stand) before the mirror since 8.30 in the morning; he is still there.
10. You see time and tide—(wait) for none for centuries. Will it wait for us today?
11. Long ago, the tortoise—(beat) the hare in a race.
12. Minutes after it died, the Phoenix—(rise) from its own ashes.
13. Down human history, the slow and steady—(always win) the race.
14. The PM—(lose) the vote of confidence. So now, a mid-term election is necessary.
15. Many a rose—(bloom) and so, my garden now smells so sweet.
16. It cannot be Clare. I—(know) her for years.
17. You—(master) the multiplication tables. So, today, you are able to multiply four-digit numbers easily.
18. For the period of four years of her training, she—(perfect) the art of teaching.

{**Answers**: 1. has left 2. leapt 3. has visited 4. have never traveled; met 5. shot 6. sprang 7. has flown 8. has flowed; blessed. 9. has stood. 10. has waited 11. beat 12. rose 13.have always won 14. has lost 15. has bloomed 16. have known 17. have mastered 18. has perfected}

3.3 CONDITIONALS

Who will survive?

The class is divided into, say 5 groups. Each group picks up a paper strip with the profession written on—carpenter, farmer, teacher, sweeper, doctor and so on.

Now, assume that these five people are aboard a helicopter, which is about to crash within 5 minutes. There is only one parachute for escape. Each person argues that he is the most important and most useful to humanity and so must be allowed to use the parachute.

Each group can discuss strong points for its representative in the helicopter. They come to the front and argue:

"If I am not allowed to escape, people will starve because they won't have food materials to eat." and so on

---

FOR TEACHERS TO THINK ABOUT

1. Conditional clauses can be introduced, besides 'If', by 'unless,' 'whether', 'provided', 'on condition that', 'So long as', 'whatever'
2. The same tenses, present or past, can be used in conditionals to show cause and effect or scientific truths. (No.4 in the table given in the beginning of the section)
3. 'Should ' is used in the if-clause to suggest doubt:
   Eg: If the Chief Guest should come late, we will have to wait till then. (The speaker feels that the Guest won't be late.)
4. The above sentence, and for that matter all such conditionals, can be accepted without the conjunction:
   Should the Chief Guest come late, -----
   Had she looked in the drawer,-------

First, study the following table:

Type of condition	If-clause	Main clause	Remarks
1. Open	If she gets time	she will do it	reference to future
2. Rejected/Imaginary in the present	If he were here	we would discuss the matter	he is not here
3. Rejected/Imaginary in the past	If he had been here	we would have discussed it.	—
4. Scientific condition	If I eat too much cheese	it gives me in-digestion	—

Use the suitable form of the verbs in the brackets:
1. If I—(sell) this house, I should get a good amount.
2. What would you do if you—(miss) the last bus?
3. I could never have solved the mystery if you—(not help) me.
4. If only we—(be) two miRstes earlier, we should have caught the train.
5. We will have the match if the weather—(be) fine
6. If I—(be) an elephant, I would let you ride on my back.

7. I—(enjoy) the poem if it hadn't been too long.
8. He will not listen to you even if you—(talk) to him.
9. We would be glad if the shopkeepers—(stick) to the MRP.
10. She would have come if she—(have) a car.
11. If they save money, they—(become) rich.
12. If she—(be) here, she would be angry with you.
13. I would perch on your window if I—(be) a bird.
14. In winter—(come), Spring cannot be far behind.
15. If he were a lion, he—(make) leopards tame.
16. I—(take) arms against a sea of troubles, if I were made of a sterner stuff.
17. If she unmasks her beauty to the moon, she—(call) prodigal.
18. You will be regarded cruel if you—(lead) your graces to the grave leaving no copy to the world.
19. If I wrote about your beauty, the world—(call) me a liar.
20. If you are woman born, my life—(not yield) to you.
21. I would compare her to unsunned snow if I—(be) to described her.
22. If I cannot be won, I—(die) as chaste as Diana.
23. If I were a woman, I—(love) you more than all the 'mores'.
24. If it—(be) a hot day, we would brandish nothing but a bottle.
25. If the nightingale—(be) to sing by day, she'd be thought a wren.
26. If I—(have) a thousand sons, I would first teach them to addict themselves to sack.
27. If I—(get) his handkerchief, I would kill Othello's sleep.

(**Answers:** All the answers below with 'will' can be replaced by 'shall' or 'can' or 'may' or vice versa. Similarly, 'would', 'should', 'could' and 'might' are equivalents in the answers.)

{1. Sold 2. Missed 3. Had not helped 4. Had been 5. Is 6. Was/Were 7. Would/should/could/might have enjoyed 8. Talk 9. Stuck 10. Had had 11. Will/Shall become 12. Were/was 13. Was/Were 14. Comes 15. Would/should/could/might make 16. Would /could . . . 17. Can be/will be . . . 18. Lead 19. Would call . . . 20. will not/ shall not/Cannot yield 21. Was/Were 22. I shall/will die 23. Would/ Should/Might love 24. Was/Were 25. Was/were 26. Had 27. Got }

Final test on the use of tenses

A. Supply the correct form of the verb in brackets, going by the context in each question:
1. I could run faster, if I (be)—a deer.
2. Here—(go) the second and the third shots.
3. As I crossed the bridge, I saw the fisherman—(swim); I don't know whether he crossed the river or not.
4. I saw the man—(swim); he soon reached the shore and talked to me
5. —trainees—(know) that plagiarism is an offence?
6. If you—(win) the first prize, what might you feel?
7. If she—(creep) always, she would injure herself.
8. I—(row) the boat along the river that—(flow) gently.
9. He—(be) smart since he—(score) in the National Games
10. We—(admit) to this college in 1996 and—(study) here ever since.

11. If I—(sell) this house, I should get a good amount.
12. What would you do if you—(miss) the last bus?
13. I could never have solved the mystery if you—(not help) me.
14. These days, prices—(shoot) up unnoticed.
15. All I know is that a swallow never—(make) spring.
16. He will apologize when good sense—(prevail)
17. I—(know) him for ten years now.
18. We—(have) our lunch when you visited us.
19. A cat came in when I—(teach).
20. My house has no roof now. The roof—(blow) off by the wind.
21. He shook hands with me and—(bid) farewell.
22. Jack, see how the student—(defy) his teacher.
23. When I—(be) seventy, your son will probably be ten.
24. In fact, the bear—(withdraw) into the forest when the forest guard came.
25. It—(rain) when we stopped at Bangalore for tea.
26. Sudan—(grow) in leaps and bounds ever since I came here.
27. If wishes were horses, beggars—(ride) them.
28. Every day last week, my daughter—(lose) a pencil.
29. What to do? The bus—(leave). We reached late.
30. Many countries—(not manage) to abolish corruption for years now.

{**Answers:** 1. were/ was 2. go 3. swimming 4. swim 5. Do/ know 6. won 7. crept 8. row/rowed; flows/flowed 9. has been/ scored 10. were admitted; have studied 11. sold 12. missed 13. had not helped 14. shoot 15. makes 16. prevails 17. have known 18. were having 19. was teaching 20. has been blown 21. bade 22. Is defying/ defies 23. Am/ become 24. Had withdrawn 25. Was raining 26. Has grown/ has been growing 27. Would/could/ should/might ride 28. lost 29. Had left 30. Have not managed}

B. Use the correct verb in the right form, as suggested by those in brackets. Write only the answers.

Today unemployment once again—1—(become) a hard fact of economic life, even in the developed countries of Europe and N. America. It seems—2—(haunt) us like a ghost from the past. Indeed, the problem appears so serious that some economists predict that many thousands of children who—3—(leave) school this year—4—(never get) jobs during their entire working lives.

In the year which followed the II World War, governments pursued full employment policies which ensured a small reserve of labour—5—(remain) idle. At that time, the mass unemployment which some experienced in the 1930s—6—(think) to be a thing of the past which—7—(not happen) again. Even when the Rsmbers out of work increased during the 1970s, most people—8—(expect) only a temporary recession—9—(bring about) by external factors like the oil crisis.

Now, however, many believe that automation and the changed structure of world trade –10—(reduce) permanently the amount of labour required by the industrial countries.

{Answers: 1. has become 2. to haunt 3. leave 4. will never get 5. to remain 6. was thought 7. would not 8. expected 9. to be brought about 10. will reduce}

C. Use the correct verb in the right form, as suggested by those in brackets. Write only the answers.
As the applause—1 (sound) all around, Alison—2(smile) widely and—3(look) straight into the eyes
of his Maths teacher. "What—4(make) you smile, Alison?" he—5(ask). "Not what you—6(study)
surely. Trignometry rarely—7(inspire) a smile as wide as yours." Alison—8(sigh). If only she—9(have)
an opportunity to sing on the MTV, she—10(be) a star today.

{**Answer**s: 1. sounded 2. smiled 3. looked 4. makes 5. asked 6. study 7. inspires 8. sighed 9. had 10.
would/ should/ could / might be}

4. QUESTION TAGS

Read the story below:

Once, there lived a sparrow with her mate on a banyan tree. One day, the sparrow laid her eggs in the nest. But soon, an elephant from the jungle came and took rest under the tree. He was unable to bear the heat of the sun and so, he broke a branch of the tree to fan himself with. Unfortunately, the sparrow's nest was on that branch. So, all her eggs were crushed and destroyed. "The elephant must respect our lives too, <u>mustn't it</u>? These big animals hardly think about us, small ones, **do they**? . . ." the he-sparrow screamed a hundred questions in pain. The he-sparrow and the she-sparrow fluttered around their broken dreams – the eggs.

A woodpecker, a close friend of theirs, comforted them, "I'm sorry. As a matter of fact, we, little creatures are helpless sometimes, **aren't we**? Don't worry. Worry always makes us weak, <u>doesn't it</u>? I have a friend – a fly, who would definitely help us to kill the elephant."

The three friends went to the fly. The fly, after considering the matter, said, "Let's work together, <u>shall we</u>? I shall introduce you to a frog—a clever, dear friend of mine. All the five of us will work together against this giant bully. Our working together will definitely defeat him, <u>won't it</u>? Let's try," the fly sounded too confident for his size.

The frog greeted them to his small pond. Sitting coolly and looking at the four friends as seriously as the headman of the village, he said, "Come on. What can an elephant do before the united strength of the five of us? Listen to me and do as I tell you, <u>will you</u>?. Mr. Fly, you used to hum sweet music in your leisure, <u>didn't you</u>? Now, use your singing talent. Go to the elephant when it is really hot and then, sing softly in his ears. He will close his eyes in delight, <u>won't he</u>? Then our woodpecker will scoop his eyes out. When this bind elephant gets thirsty, he will look for water. I will start croaking from a marsh near him. Thinking that there is water, the elephant will come there. He has heavy legs, <u>hasn't he</u>? They will sink into the marsh and the elephant-bully will at last die there."

All of them nodded in delight. The frog said, "Nodding alone is not enough. Now, get into action, won't you?"

The next day, they did as they had decided and the elephant died in the marsh.

The sets of words underlined in the story above are called *Question tags*. Question tags are used to confirm information or to fine check already confirmed information. We use the *rising intonation* for the former and a *falling intonation* for the latter.

For example,
    The classes ended at 4.00, did N'T THEY?
    Richard never comes on time, does he ?

The question tags have the following parts:

, + auxiliary verb (n't) + pronoun + ?
(small letter beginning)

The short form of 'not' i.e. 'n't' is used to make the question tag negative if only the preceding statement is positive. The negative words that make the statement negative comprise: *no, not, never, neither, nor, scarcely, hardly, rarely, seldom* and *only etc.*

Statement	Auxiliary (n't)	Pronoun?
1. The elephant must respect our lives too	, mustn't	it?
2. These big animals hardly think about us, small ones	,do	they?
3. We, little creatures are helpless sometimes.	, aren't	we?
4. Worry always makes us weak	, doesn't	it?
5. Let's work together	, shall	we?
6. Our working together will definitely defeat him	, won't	it?
7. Listen to me and do as I tell you	, will.	you?
8. You used to hum sweet music in your leisure	, didn't	you?
9. He will close his eyes in delight	, won't	he?
10. He has heavy legs	, hasn't	he?
11. Now, get into action	, won't	you?

Notice the pronouns used:

Subject	Pronouns
1. The elephant	it
2. These big animals	they
3. We	we
4. Worry	it
5. Us (We)	we
6. Our working together	it
7. You (imperative)	you
8. You	you
9. He	he
10. He	he
11. You (imperative)	you

Some special question tags

Example	**Explanation**
1. I am the youngest of the brothers, <u>aren't I ?</u>	<u>'am I ?'</u> and <u>'aren't I?'</u> are the tags with 'am'
2. One rarely suspects oneself, <u>does one?</u>	'One' is repeated as the pronoun
3. One of the girls returned, <u>didn't she?</u>	Here, the subject though is 'One' is 'she'

1.   In the sentence: *One of the boys returned*

The subject is not 'one', but 'one of the boys'. So the tag takes 'he' in the pronominal place.

One of the boys returned, didn't he?

2.   Generally, the finite verb 'have' indicates possession or something related to possession. In this case, the question tag takes 'have' itself as the auxiliary. However, if the meaning is something other than possession, we use the hidden auxiliary as before.

Examples: **Possession**
Ann hasn't many friends, has she?
Students have their own dictionaries, haven't they?

Other than possession
My mother had a bath, didn't she?
He has a letter from the boss, doesn't he?
I had breakfast, didn't I?
But, what about the 'have' in: *Ruth has worked hard, hasn't she?*

Here, 'has' is an auxiliary verb and so the tag follows the usual pattern.

The other special cases are shown in the table below:

Description	Tag	Examples
3. Beginning in 'Let's'	Shall we?	1. Let's go walking, shall we? 2. Let's not discuss the issue, shall we? 3. Let's have a cup of tea, shall we?
4. Imperatives such as order, request, advice, offer, warning and instruction etc.	Will you? (usual) Won't you? (urgency) Can't you? (Impatience)	Have plenty of milk, will you? Don't smoke any more, won't you? Switch off the light, can't you? Mind your head, will you? Boil it for 5 minutes, will you?
5. Beginning in 'I am'	Aren't I?	1. I am older than you, aren't I? 2. I am what I think, aren't I?
Beginning in 'Everybody' and 'None of..'	The pronoun is 'they'	1. Everybody hates him, don't they? 2. Everyone can't go, can they? 3. None of the students came, did they?

We also come across question tags such as:
1. I think it rained heavily, didn't it ? (not 'don't I?) (**The focus is the 'rain', not 'think'**)
2. So, you trust the text books, do you? (not 'don't you') (**The person's 'trust'ing the text books is more or less confirmed and so a negative tag is not necessary further**)
3. Beware of dogs, then! (**has the force of a formal question tag**)
4. It is really cold, mind ! (**do**)
5. You cannot stay here for long, right ? (**do**)
6. Terrible noise, isn't it? (**Informally, the auxiliary & subject are omitted**)
7. Doing well, are you? (**do**)

<u>In a nutshell</u>

- The question tag starts with a comma and ends with a question mark.
- The question tag has a suitable helping verb, followed by the short form of 'n't' if the statement is positive.
- The appropriate pronoun is used in the tag.
- 'has/have' is retained in the tag if it denotes possession; the forms of 'do' are used if it denotes other than possession.
- Imperatives take in the tag 'will you?'/'won't you?'/ 'can't you?'

Supply appropriate question tags to the following sentences:
1. Good people speak well of others.
2. Prayers from the heart seldom go wasted.
3. Everyone improves through practice.
4. Cultivate good habits.
5. I am talking as per the instructions.
6. Cinderella had a humble heart.
7. The office orders clarify your doubt.
8. Cowards die many times before their deaths.
9. None will pass the exams but the intelligent.
10. Good fences make good neighbours.
11. Give no more orders to the servants.
12. After a while, the gods chose him the new king.
13. Let us practise what we preach.
14. None embraces in their graves.
15. The Guru could hardly cast the spirit out.
16. Let's finish the homework.
17. Your painting needs better shading.
18. We shall clean our toilet regularly.
19. The children hadn't had their dinner.
20. Laziness will rust your smartness.
21. Stand in front of the class.
22. One must not live to eat.
23. Snowstorms used to destroy the crops.
24. One of the mothers had a letter from the Ministry.
25. A light wife makes a heavy husband.

{**Answers:** 1. don't they? 2. do they? 3. don't they? 4. will you? 5. aren't I? 6. hadn't she? 7. don't they? 8. don't they? 9. will they? 10. don't they? 11. can't you? 12. didn't they? 13. shall we? 14. do they? 15. could he? 16. shall we? 17. doesn't it? 18. shan't we? 19. did they? 20. won't it? 21. will you? 22. must one? 23. didn't they? 24. didn't she? 25. doesn't she?}

5. SIMPLE, COMPOUND AND COMPLEX SENTENCES

Read the story below and study the different kinds of sentences used in it.

Uncle Sam was a big businessman. However, in a strange reversal of fortune, he gradually suffered losses. *He sold all his belongings and thus was left with just an iron balance. He approached a good friend of his, Timothy and requested him to keep the balance until he returned from a pilgrimage.*

When he finished his trip, he requested for the balance. But, Timothy said that the balance had been eaten by some mice. Uncle Sam kept quiet. **Then he requested Timothy to send his son with him to a nearby river so that the boy could accompany him in the religious rites he would perform there.** His request was readily granted. *On their way, Uncle Sam pushed the boy into a cave and shut the cave with a huge stone.* **When he returned he reported to the boy's father that a hawk had carried the boy away.** Timothy was angry. **How can a hawk carry a grown-up boy? he wondered.** Uncle Sam explained that if mice ate iron, hawks would carry children, big or small.

Timothy got the message, therefore he returned the balance. **No sooner did the balance reach his hands than Uncle Sam released the boy from the cave.**

Notice that the sentences in normal font are simple; those in italics are compound and those in bold font are complex. Now, analyse them following the details given below.

SIMPLE

1.	Kate sang well.	(the only one finite verb–*sang*)
2.	Kate got the first prize.	(the only one finite verb–*got*)
3.	Uncle Sam was a big businessman.	(the only finite verb–*was*)

COMPOUND

1.	Kate sang well and she got the first prize.	(**finite verbs** – *sang, got*)
		(Co-ordinating conjunction – *and*)
2.	Kate sang well, so she got the first prize.	(do)
		(Co-ordinating conjunction – *but*)

3. He sold all his belongings and thus was left with just an iron balance.
    (**finite verbs**–*sold, was;* Co-ordinating conjunction – *and thus*

• Kate sang well. • And s/he got the first prize.	*They can stand alone (independent)*
	They are parts of a long sentence and so they are <u>*clauses.*</u>
	So, they are called CO-ORDINATE CLAUSES.

('but', 'yet', 'still', 'and', 'so', 'therefore' are some co-ordinating conjunctions)

COMPLEX

1. As Kate sang well, she got the first prize.
2. Kate sang so well that she got the first prize.
3. Kate sang well so that she could get the first prize.
4. Though Kate sang well, she did not get the first prize.
5. If Kate sang well, she would get the first prize.
6. When he finished his trip, he requested for the balance.

We can put a full stop like this:	**We cannot put a full stop like this:**
She got the first prize.	As Kate sang well. (**'As'**, **'since'** . . .)
She got the first prize.	Kate sang so well that. (**'so . . . that**)
She could get the first prize.	Kate sang well so that. (**' so that'**)
She did not get the first prize.	Though Kate sang well. (**'[al]though'**)
She would get the first prize.	If Kate sang well. (**'If'** , **'In case'**)
They are MAIN CLAUSES / PRINCIPAL CLAUSES/ INDEPENDENT CLAUSES	**They are SUBORDINATE CLAUSES/ DEPENDENT CLAUSES**

Let's sum up:	
ONE FINITE VERB **Simple**	**TWO/MORE FINITE VERBS** ***Compound ('but', 'and', 'so' etc.)** ***Complex ('As', 'Though', 'If' etc.)**

Jose K . C

Exercise: Practise, by grouping the following sentences into *Simple, Compound* and *Complex:*
1. Mark is a teacher and a pianist.
2. Lucy is so clever that she cannot miss the point.
3. William walked daily so that he might keep himself fit.
4. Martin walked daily for fitness.
5. Raju walked daily in order to keep himself fit.
6. Robert walks daily, still he is sickly.
7. This is the kite that Ruth made.
8. The Principal told us to keep quiet.
9. The Principal told us that we should keep quiet.
10. Though we shouted, our teacher kept quiet.
11. In spite of our disobedience, our teacher kept quiet.
12. Poets are born, but orators are made.
13. Though poets are born, orators are made.
14. Cinderella left the dance at the stroke of the bell.
15. Cinderella left the dance when the bell struck twelve.
16. Cinderella left the dance because of the bell.
17. The bell struck twelve, therefore Cinderella left the dance.
18. A thing of beauty is a joy forever.
19. A thing that is beautiful is a joy forever.
20. It's a thing of beauty, so it is a joy forever.
21. If the thing is beautiful, it can give us joy.
22. We are such stuff that dreams are made of.
23. We and dreams are made of the same stuff.
24. We are made of dreamy stuff.
25. If music is the food of love, play on.

{**Answers:** 4, 5,8,11,14,18, 23, 24simple; 1, 6, 12, 17, 20 compound; 2 3,7, 9,10,13, 15, 16,19, 21, 22, 25 complex}

In a nutshell

* One finite verb = simple
* two or more finite verbs = either compound or complex
* 'and', 'but', 'yet' and 'therefore' etc. may indicate a compound sentence.
* 'since', 'if', 'though', 'so that' and 'whether' etc. may indicate a complex sentence.

Convert the following into simple sentences:

1. He did not attend the meeting because he was sick.
2. He was advised repeatedly, still he misbehaved.
3. Music is the food of love; so, you play on.
4. As he had been humiliated publicly, he wept bitterly.
5. She is so clever that she cannot bear a long-winding explanation.
6. Kate's daughter eloped with her lover and that was much to his disappointment.
7. A stone that rolls cannot gather moss.

44

{**Answers:** 1. He did not attend the meeting because of sickness.
2. Despite repeated advice, he misbehaved.
3. You play on music, the food of love.
4. Having been humiliated in public, he wept bitterly.
5. She is too clever to bear a long-winding explanation.
6. Much to his disappointment, Kate's daughter eloped with her lover.
7. A rolling stone gathers no moss.}

6. VOICE CHANGE

Read the story and pay special attention to the sentences which are underlined:

Once, the lion of the forest was suffering from severe indigestion. His subjects visited him one by one and tried their home-made medicines. He was not cured, however.

When the zebra came, he sniffed around to detect the nature of indigestion. He then commented, "Your Majesty, what a foul breath you have got! You must have a serious problem."
"How dare you?" the lion roared and knocked the zebra down. Seeing honesty had been killed, the approaching hyena praised the lion. He expected some rewards too. "Your Majesty, you breathe so sweetly even in illness."

The lion did not like the obvious flattery in the hyena's words. "You foolish sycophant!! You took me for a fool? Your words are given what they deserve." Though sick, the lion pounced on the poor flatterer and slaughtered him.

The fox, who was behind a bush, came forward and bowed before the ailing king. The lion, still angry, expected a similar flattery from him. "What do you think, little one? How does my breath feel?"

"Your Majesty, I am unable to judge it as my nostrils are blocked." The lion nodded his head and left him alone. Prudence was the best companion – the other animals learned.

SPECIAL NOTE.

1. The active voice is simple, natural and warm. The passive voice is used when the situation so demands. We use the passive voice when:
> - **The doer is unknown or unimportant.** (Someone knocked at the door =The door was knocked at.)
> - **We want to highlight the action done to the object.** (They hide facts =Facts are hidden.)

In passive voice, we use any one of these verb patterns:

1. **BE + PP** (PP = Past participle, ie. the 3rd form as in 'write'—'wrote'—'written')
2. **BE + being + PP**
3. **Has/Have/Had + been + PP**
('BE' is any one of 'am', 'is', 'was', 'are', 'were' and
'Has' and 'Have' are in present tense and 'Had' in past; 'Has' is *singular and 'Have' plural.)

Consider the following examples:
    A congratulates B (Start : B . . .)
Ans: B is congratulated by A. (Notice that we have used the first verb pattern : BE +PP. Why ? The answer is in the examples given below:

Active voice	*Passive voice*
A is congratulating	B B is being congratulated by A
A has congratulated	B B has been congratulated by A

That means : there is 'be+pp' in all passive sentences ('being congratulated' and 'been congratulated'). Notice that the '-ing' in the active voice is repeated in the 'being' in the passive voice and the past participle ('congratulated') in the active is repeated in the #'been' in the passive. And, the 'congratulated'

For inquisitive minds: *Generally, the 's-ending' in verbs shows they are singular (eg. 'does', 'has', 'eats' and 'carries' etc., but the 's-ending' in nouns plural (eg. 'boys' and 'mangoes' etc.). # We need pp after 'has' and be before the 'pp' – 'congratulated'. Hence 'been'.

Note: 1.When there is an *extra word or phrase in the active, it is often put just after the 'PP' in the passive. For example :

Active	Passive
A congratulates B publicly.	B is congratulated publicly by A.
(extra word)	(PP) (extra word)

2. When there are #two objects in the active, either can be taken as the subject in the passive. Here, the other object will be treated as the 'extra word/phrase' as stated above. For example :
Active Passive

Active	Passive
1. He gives me a pen.	a. I am given a pen by him.
object-1	b. A pen is given to me by him.
object –2	(Notice the use of 'to' after the 'PP' only in 'b', not in 'a'.)
2. They offer her a chair.	a. She is offered a chair (by them.)
	b. A chair is offered to her (by them.)

(NB: The 'agent phrase' – i.e. 'by them' – is shown in brackets just to tell the students that all 'agent phrases' can be omitted in the passive.)

3. The phrasal verbs (= verbs in the form of phrases) change in their wholeness/entirety. In other words, the preposition or the adverbial particle after the verb should also go to the passive.

Active: He put the shirt <u>on</u>.   Passive: The shirt was put <u>on</u> (by him).

 For inquisitive minds: *Generally, if the extra word is an adverb like 'often', 'never' and 'seldom' etc., it comes next to the 'be'/ 'have' in the passive. E.g. *Geniuses are often misunderstood.*

 #Those verbs in English that can govern two objects are called **ditransitive** verbs. E.g. *teach, offer, tell . . .*

 @ Prepositions always come before the object and, adverbial particle often after the object and always after the pronoun object. E.g. *look after the baby (Prep.), lock the shop up* (or *lock up the shop*) and always *lock it up* (adv.particle).

Active	Passive
The teacher gave him a reward.	a. He was given a reward (by . . .) b. A reward was given to him(by . . .)
Her absence disturbs me sometimes.	I am disturbed sometimes(by her absence.)
They are showing us great hospitality	a. We are being shown great hosp. . . . b. Great hospitality is being shown to us (by . . . .)
Those miscreants have picked my pocket.	My pocket has been picked(by those miscre-ants.)
All my sisters encouraged me loudly.	I was encouraged loudly (by all my . . .)
People have chosen him the chief.	He has been chosen the chief (by . . .)
Angels don't tread on his path.	His path isn't trodden on (by angels.)
She/He sheds crocodile tears.	Crocodile tears are shed (by her/him.)
You don't collect grapes from thistles.	Grapes aren't collected from thistles (by you/ anyone)
He didn't drive my car.	My car wasn't driven (by him.)
She bears the misfortunes silently.	The misfortunes are borne silently(by..)
We have beaten them in the debate.	They have been beaten in the debate..

The dog bit a few teenagers.	A few teenagers were bitten by the dog
The wind blows off the roofs.	The roofs are blown off by the wind.
They are broadcasting the news.	The news is being broadcast by them.
She has clung to a religious belief.	A religious belief has been clung to by her.
He had not dreamt of a girl.	A girl had not been dreamt of by him.
We were feeding the dog with meat.	The dog was being fed with meat by us
I fly the aircraft solo.	The aircraft is flown solo by me.
He will have ground the rice by now.	The rice will have been ground by now.

In a Rstshell

- 'be + past participle' is the basic structure of the passive voice. 'being' is added to this structure in case of a contiRsous tense and 'been' in case of a perfect tense.
- In case of two objects (following ditransitive verbs), each object is treated separately in the passive conversion. The second object is placed just after the past particple.
- Passive voice is used on formal occasions and is more impersonal in effect. Active voice is preferred in personal, informal situations.

Exercises

Put the following sentences into passive voice :

1. The snowfall destroys the crops.
2. They sent for the priests.
3. The clerk reserves us three seats.
4. Corbett shot the man-eater down.
5. Mother Teresa raised hopes in the sagging minds.
6. He was winning applause.
7. The goddess has thrown an apple of discord.
8. Nobody thought over the side effects.
9. Over-use wears out the surface.
10. My young sister tore my skirt.

More challenging ones.

11. Words pay no debts.
12. Lions make leopards tame.
13. He has brought many captives home.
14. Nature teaches beasts to know their friends.
15. Misery acquaints a man with strange bed-fellows.
16. The raven crocks the fatal entrance of Duncan

17. He that dies pays all debts.
18. Divinity shapes our ends.
19. The apparel often proclaims the man.
20. Men don't put a lighted candle under a bushel
21. The letter kills but the spirit gives life.
22. Despair has often gained battles.
23. The richest soil, if uncultivated, produces the rankest weeds
24. Pain forces even the innocent to lie
25. Little words never hurt a big idea.
{Answers: 1.The crops are destroyed by the snowfall.
2. The priests were sent for.
3. Three seats are reserved for us by the clerk.
4. The man-eater was shot down (by Corbett.)
5. Hopes were raised in the sagging minds (by Mother Teresa.)
6. Applause was being won (by him.)
7. An apple of discord has been thrown.
8. The side effects were not thought over (by anybody.)
9. The surface is worn out by over-use.
10. My skirt was torn (by my young sister.)
11. No debts are paid by words.
12. Leopards are made tame by lions.
13. Many captives have been brought home by him.
14. Beasts are taught to know their friends (by Nature.)
15. A man is acquainted with strange bed-fellows (by misery.)
16. The fatal entrance of Duncan is crocked by the raven.
17. All debts are paid by him who (that) dies.
18. Our ends are shaped by divinity.
19. The man is often proclaimed by the apparel.
20. A lighted candle is not put under a bushel.
21. Life is killed by the letter but given by the spirit.
22. Battles have often been gained by despair.
23. The rankest weeds are produced by the richest soil, if . . .
24. Even the innocent are forced to lie (by pain.)
25. A big idea is never hurt by little words.}

Use the correct passive forms of the verbs in brackets, along with the appropriate prepositions. Write only the answers.

Eg: The child that—(run) was seriously injured. Answer: was run over

My dear son, please listen to me before you leave for a distant land. First, don't be talkative and don't speak unless you—1—(speak). Remember, once in your office, you—2—(pay) the work you do, every month. In other words, the quality of the work, which—3—(attend) by you is what matters. The kinds of work, which you—4—(ask) by your boss depend on the Board's decisions. Mind you, my son, be at your boss's side without much delay every time you—5—(send).

{Answers:
1. are spoken to
2. are /will be/ get paid for
3. is attended to
4. are/ will be asked (for)
5. are sent for}

6.1 VOICE CHANGE IN QUESTIONS.

Basically, there is no difference in the procedure and the verb patterns used while changing the voice of questions (or interrogative sentences) from those mentioned above. But we should remember to retain the *inversion, which is a characteristic of almost all questions. To illustrate:

He <u>has been working hard.</u>   (Statement)
   V1 V2 V3
<u>Has he been working</u> hard ?   (Question)
   V1 V2 V3

Here, ' V1-V2—V3' is the *verb phrase.* Notice that V1 in the question is before the subject, 'he', whereas it is after 'he' in the statement. This is inversion. (Exceptions: 'Who wrote the book?' and 'What caused the fire?' etc.)

Let us consider the first example in this unit:
     Does A congratulate B ? (active)
     Is B congratulated by A ? (passive). Notice that we have retained the inversion, by keeping the V1 ie. 'Is' before the subject, 'B'.

(Please note that the passive change exercise is done below in order to show how a passive construction is possible. In fact, many of the passive sentences in the right columns below are unnecessary and at times awkward to use in day-to-day communications. In such cases, students are earnestly advised to use the active voice.)

Active	Passive
Does Linda write poems regularly ?	Are poems written regularly by Linda ?
Do plants bear flowers in winter ?	Are flowers borne in winter (by plants?)
Is Tom whitewashing the fence ?	Is the fence being whitewashed (by Tom ?)
Have you won the bet ?	Has the bet been won (by you ?)
Were they going through my homework?	Was my homework being gone through by them ?

| Will they have finished the work by 17th ? | Will the work have been finished by 17th (by them ?) |
| Does a thing of beauty give us joy for-ever? | a. Are we given joy for ever by a thing of beauty?/b. Is joy for . . . . ? |

¹What caused his anger?	What was his anger caused by?
²What are they discussing?	What is being discussed (by them?)
³What power has brought you here?	By what power have you been brought here? / What . . . . by?
⁴What are you talking about?	What is being talked about . . . ?
⁵Why had he written off the debts?	Why had the debts been written off (by him?)
Who taught you grammar?	Who are you taught grammar by? /By whom are . . . ?/ Who is grammar taught to you by? etc.
Whom did you meet yesterday?	Who was met yesterday by you?
Which book do you refer to?	Which book is referred to(by you?)
What have you depended on?	What has been depended on (by you?)
Who wrote <u>Pygmalion</u> ?	Who was <u>Pygmalion</u> written by ?
Why have they ill-timed the operation?	Why has the operation been ill-timed (by them?)

For inquisitive minds: *Inversion is the word order of 'verb first – subject second' in most of the questions and sentences beginning in negative words such as 'never', 'hardly', 'seldom' and so on. For instance, in sentences such as 'Where have you been ?' and 'Never have I been to Delhi', the first part of the verb phrase (V1) ie. 'have' is before the subjects – 'you' and 'I' respectively.

For inquisitive minds: 1—5 The question words such as these (ie. 'What', 'why' and 'how' etc.) function in different ways. The question word acts as the subject, the object, an adjective, the object of a preposition and an adverb in Nos. 1, 2, 3, 4 and 5 respectively. In fact, this knowledge can smoothen the voice change exercise.

Exercises: Put the following sentences into passive:
1. What are you looking at?
2. Who leaves the work incomplete?
3. Where have they hidden the treasure?
4. Who started the engine?
5. Why do we fear the unborn tomorrow?

6. How can they bear the blame?
7. Is she raking up the old scandals?
8. Did you bring the dictionary?

<u>More challenging ones</u>
1. Has he laughed off my suggestions?
2. Will Tom have briefed us about it by 10 tomorrow?
3. Need you waste so many words on this topic?
4. Who is he referring to?
5. Where can one find a suitable lodge?
6. Were they selling off their name?
7. How does value-erosion wreck peoples?
      (Here *peoples = nations*)

{**Answers:** 1.What is being looked at (by you?)
2. Who is the work left incomplete by? OR
By whom is the work left incomplete?
3. Where has the treasure been hidden (by them?)
4. Who was the engine started by?
5. Why is the unborn tomorrow feared (by us?)
6. How can the blame be borne by them?
7. Are the old scandals being raked up by her?
8. Was the dictionary brought by you?

1. Have my suggestions been laughed at (by him?)
2. Shall we have been briefed about it by 10 tomorrow . . .
3. Need so many words be wasted on this topic (by you?)
4. Who is/are being referred to (by him?)
5. Where can a suitable lodge be found?
6. Was their name being sold off?
7. How are peoples wrecked by value-erosion?}

6.2 VOICE CHANGE IN IMPERATIVES AND AUXILIARIES

The passive voice in the imperatives (request, command and advice etc.)
is introduced with 'Let', as :
1. Write the essay carefully. (Active)
Let the essay be written carefully. (Passive)
2. Don't forget the consequences. (Active)
Let not the consequences be forgotten. (Passive)
3. Don't tax him with extra work. (Active)
Let him not be taxed with . . . . (Passive)

> **Note :** *'not' is placed after 'him'(in No.3 Passive) because the latter is a 'personal object' and otherwise, before the object ('the consequences') as in No.2 Passive.*

VOICE CHANGE IN AUXILIARIES.

The main verbs (such as 'will take', 'must finish' and 'ought to write' etc.) containing the auxiliaries such as 'will', 'shall', 'may', 'might', 'must' and 'can' etc.(ie. 'aux.+infinitive') are changed into the passive just by adding 'be +PP'. For example:

He will win laurels. (Active)

Laurels will be won by him. (Passive)

Those in glass houses must not throw stones. (Active)

Stones must not be thrown by those . . . . OR

Stones must not be thrown from glass houses.

*Notice the change of 'will' into 'shall' in the following example:

They will treat me well. (Active)

I shall be treated well . . . . (Passive)

Why this change? The answer is: *'will' is with the third person – they – and 'shall' is with the first person – I.*

Exercises: Put the following sentences into passive:
1. Dismiss him off your mind.
2. Clean the floor fast.
3. Throw away the residue.
4. Weigh his points against his experience.
5. Cast off your vinegar disposition.
6. Don't fertilize the corn-ear.
7. Fly the plane solo.
8. Ring out miseries.
9. Sow seeds in well-tilled soil.
10. Write off his debts.

More challenging ones
11. Plough your mind first.
12. Unsex Lady Macbeth instantly.
13. Whitewash the grave in her.
14. Don't wear borrowed garments.
15. Bear not duties half-willingly.
16. Assume a virtue (even) if you have it not.
17. Call a spade a spade.
18. Mark her absent.
19. Advertise the vacancy.
20. Remove the log from your eyes.
21. Wind up your speech.
22. Don't bear false testimony.

23. Stop him from philosophizing.
24. 24. Don't cast your pearls before the swine.
25. 25. Leave the dead to bury their own dead.
26. Don't kick against the prick.
27. Give Caesar what is Caesar's.
28. Bid all latecomers to my office.
29. Reap what you sow.
30. Mar no more trees with love-songs.

{Answers: 1.Let him be dismissed off your mind.
2. Let the floor be cleaned fast.
3. Let the residue be thrown away.
4. Let his points be weighed against his experiences.
5. Let your vinegar disposition be cast off.
6. Let not the corn-ear be fertilized.
7. Let the plane be flown solo.
8. Let miseries be rung out.
9. Let seeds be sown in well-tilled soil.
10. Let his debts be written off.
11. Let your mind be ploughed first.
12. Let Lady Macbeth be unsexed instantly.
13. Let the grave in her be whitewashed.
14. Let not borrowed garments be worn.
15. Let not duties be borne half-willingly.
16. Let a virtue be assumed (even) if you have it not.
17. Let a spade be called a spade.
18. Let her be marked absent.
19. Let the vacancy be advertised.
20. Let the log be removed from your eyes.
21. Let your speech be wound up.
22. Let not false testimony be borne.
23. Let him be stopped from philosophizing.
24. Let not your pearls be cast before the swine.
25. Let the dead be left to bury their own dead.
26. Let not the prick be kicked against.
27. Let Caesar be given what is Caesar's.
28. Let all latecomers be bidden to my office.
29. Let what you sow be reaped.
30. Let no more trees be marred with love-songs.}

6.3   DOUBLE PASSIVE

When the main verb in a sentence and an infinitive in it are put in the passive, we get the double passive. For example:

1. The Officer commanded us to shoot the thief. (Active)
   We were commanded to shoot the thief. (Single passive)
   The thief was commanded to be shot. (Double passive)
2. I saw the boy *kick the dog. (Active)
   The boy was seen to kick the dog. (Single passive)
   The dog was seen (to be) kicked. (Double passive)

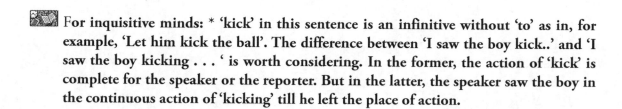 **For inquisitive minds: * 'kick' in this sentence is an infinitive without 'to' as in, for example, 'Let him kick the ball'. The difference between 'I saw the boy kick..' and 'I saw the boy kicking . . . ' is worth considering. In the former, the action of 'kick' is complete for the speaker or the reporter. But in the latter, the speaker saw the boy in the continuous action of 'kicking' till he left the place of action.**

> **However, the following double passive constructions are wrong:**
> # The tree was attempted to be climbed.
> # The bag is asked to be carried.
>
> *The reason:* **The subjects in the double passive—'The tree' and 'The bag'—cannot stand as the objects of the main verbs in the active. In other words, though one can try saying:** *Somebody attempted the tree to climb* **or** *Someone asks the bag to carry*, **they are unacceptable sentences.**

---

7. REPORTED SPEECH

While reading the story below, take note of the sentences underlined:

A salt seller had a faithful donkey, who carried his salt for sale to different towns. Gradually, the donkey grew lazy. One day he told himself, "I shall pretend today to be sick." Unfortunately, the salt merchant heard these words. He decided to advise his donkey. However, he was so busy that he forgot it for a week. After a week, he went near the donkey and asked him, "Did you say that you would pretend to be sick?"

"No, Sir. I haven't even thought of that."

"Well, then; it's good for you. Today, I have two sacks of salt. Get ready to take them."

In fact, the donkey was very sad. But, there was no way out.

While on the way, they had to wade through a small river. The donkey suddenly got an idea. He pretended that he was tumbling on a stone and fell into the river. Much of the salt dissolved in the water and thus his load became light.

The merchant saw through the donkey's plan and decided to teach him a lesson. The next day, <u>he told the donkey that he had two sacks of salt that day too</u>. The donkey nodded his head and carried them on his back. In fact, it was cotton, not salt. On the way, the donkey used the same trick. But, this time, instead of losing weight, the two sacks became heavier as cotton had absorbed a good quantity of water. The donkey was surprised and sad. <u>The donkey asked his master what made the sacks heavier than before</u>. The salt seller laughed and said that it was cotton. He wanted to teach the lazy and cunning donkey a lesson.
****

Exercises in Reported speech or conversions from Direct into Indirect speech give students, especially those for whom English is a foreign language, drills in sentence structures, tense use and pronoun changes etc.

In Direct speech, the tense, the pronouns and the adverbs (called the 'deictic elements') naturally refer to the speech situation. Therefore, when that speech is reported, these deictic elements need to be changed.

Note that in the story above, "I shall pretend to be sick" became "Did you say that you would pretend to be sick?" Similarly, "…he told the donkey that he had two sacks of salt that day too" can be the reported version of "…he said to the donkey, 'I have two sacks of cotton today too.'"

Let us consider the following example:

DIRECT: "Before you reach here tomorrow," Lucy said to Andrew, "I will have boarded the train."

INDIRECT: Lucy told Andrew that before he reached there the following day, she would have boarded the train.

(NOTE: In the Direct Speech above, notice the position of the two commas and one full stop. Inverted commas – whether opening or closing – are used only after the commas and the full stop.)

Some of the important guidelines one must bear in mind while reporting include:

1. All the finite verbs within the speech marks will change:
   Present tense – to – Past tense – to – had + PP.
2. If the reporting verb is in present or future tense, retain the tenses in the speech marks as they are (a rare situation)
3. The other changes (from nearness to distance) are:

Pronoun changes				**Adverb changes**		
I,we	to	**he/she/they**		**now**	to	**then**
me, us		**him/her/them**		**this**		**that**
my, our		**his/her/their**		**these**		**those**
you(sub)		**he/she/they**		**here**		**there**
you(obj)		**him/her/them**		**ago**		**before**
your		**his/her/their**		**today**		**that day**
yours		**his/hers/theirs**		**tomorrow**		**the next/ following day**
				yesterday		**the previous day**
				tonight		**that night**
				next day		**the following**
				day last year		**the previous year**

NOTE: It is very important to use our common sense for these changes.

1. Reporting statements/declaratives/assertives

The example given earlier of Lucy's speech to Andrew serves as a good example of how to report a statement. Here, a few things can be considered:

a. If the presence of the listener is clear in the context, 'said' can be preferably changed to 'told'.
b. If the situation clearly tells us the way the speech is uttered, we would prefer other reporting verbs such as 'whispered', 'announced', 'boasted' and so on.
2. The speech marks are removed by using 'that'.
3. More examples:

1. "You have made us come all the way for nothing."
    Ruth told Richard that he had made them come all the way for nothing.

2. "My father's car is too old. We will sell it today and are planning to buy a new one," Thomas said.
    Thomas said that his father's car was too old and that they would sell it that day and were planning to buy a new one.

3. "I shall start from here at 9 tomorrow. Michael, if you want to come with me, I can take you, " Martin said.

Martin told Sangyo that he would start from there at 9 the next day. He added that if Sangyo wanted to go with him, he could take him.

(Notice the slight changes different from the usual ones. Strictly, 'shall' should change to 'should'. In the above case, the first person 'I' is changed to the third person 'he'. Therefore the first person use of 'shall' must change to the third person use of 'will'. Hence the past of it. 'would'. In the case of 'go', the situation demands the change of 'come' to 'go'. Contrast it with that of 'come' in the next example)

4. "I hope you will come to school tomorrow, " Clare said to her father.
    Clare told her father that he hoped she would come to school the following day.

5. "I don't think you will improve as you haven't shown any signs of improvement till now," the teacher said to me.
    The teacher told me that he didn't think I would improve as I hadn't shown any signs of improvement till then.

6. "I can't remember what you told me yesterday, "Tracy told her father.
    Tracy told her father that she could not remember what he had told her the previous day.

Students' problem

Some students, while reporting No.5, for example, may answer:

The teacher told me that he didn't thought …….
In No.5, the verbs, <u>didn't think</u>' and '<u>haven't shown</u>' are compound
       V1 V2   V1   V2
verbs, in which case, only V1 changes to past tense. In all such cases, V2, V3 etc are non-finites, which are unaffected by tenses. Remember the guidelines given earlier: only finite verbs change.

---

ii. Reporting questions/interrogatives

Questions, generally speaking, have the following two characteristics:

1. Verb before the subject (Eg: Where were you yesterday?)
                                 V sub
2. Beginning in a question word.
     (Eg: When did you come?

    Did I tell you that?

    The question word here is 'whether' (implicit)

Therefore, when questions are reported, we must use the question word instead of 'that' (in reported statements). Secondly, the verb order of verb-subject must become subject-verb.

Examples:
1. Ian said, "What do you want, Kevin?"
   Ian asked Kevin, what he wanted.
2. "Will you lend me a pencil?" I said to Meera.
3. "Where have you been this afternoon?" the mother to her boy. The mother asked her boy where he had been all that afternoon.
4. "My eyes itch; does that bode weeping?' Desdemona to Emil. Desdemona told Emil that her eyes itched. Shed asked Emil whether that boded weeping.
5. "Shall I compare you to a summer's day?" he said to her.
   He asked her whether he should compare her to a summer's day.
6. Brutus told the other conspirators, "What else do we need but our own cause to prick us to redress."
   Brutus asked the conspirators what else they needed but their own cause to prick them to redress.

7. "Do you think it will rain?" my mother asked me.
    My mother asked me whether I thought it would rain.

8. "When does your brother return from England/" she asked me. She asked me when my brother would return from England.

9. "Where did you go for your holiday/ "I asked him.
    I asked him where he had gone for his holiday.

10. "How many English lessons do you each week/" the tourist to us. The tourist asked us how many lessons we had each week.

For Teachers To Think About:

Why do you think the following reporting is acceptable though some of the changes (the underlined) do not conform to the rules discussed so far:

1. A: He said, "The earth goes round the sun."
    B: He said that the earth goes round the sun.
2. A: He said," The doctor returns from Canada tomorrow."
    B: She said that the doctor would return from Canada the following day.
3. A: He said, "He visits his grandma now and then."
    B: He said that he visited his grandma now and then.
4. A: Paul said, " Perm, you didn't mean it, did you?"
    B: Paul asked Perm whether he had meant it.
5. A: She said to me, "Would you please move a little?"
    B: She requested me to move a little.

** We must use a personal object after verbs such as: tell, ask, request, order, forbid, instruct, remind and so on because they show closely linked actions - either two actions done by the same person or two different persons. Such structures are called Phase Structures. Therefore, it is non-standard to say, "He tells that…."

Topic: Reporting Imperatives

Imperatives are sentences that convey orders, requests, advice, warnings, suggestions and instructions etc. Depending on the tone of the speaker, various reporting verbs can be used such as 'ordered', 'advised' 'directed', 'urged', 'warned' and so on. But the commonest are 'told' and 'asked'. Here, there is no use of a reporting conjunction (as 'that' in statements or the question word in interrogatives). Instead, the infinitive of the main verb is used.

Examples:
1. A. "Martin, open the window," his father said.
    B. His father told Martin to open the window.

2. A. "Go to your room and don't come out until you are called," my mother told me.
   B. My mother asked me to go to my room and not to come out until I was called.

(**Note**: Adverbs like 'not', 'always' and 'never' etc. should be placed before 'to')

3. A. "Don't walk on the grass, "the guard told us.
   B. The guard advised us not to walk on the grass
4. A. "Do stay with us tonight, "the children said to their uncle.
   B. The children entreated their uncle to stay with them that night.

(**Note**: 'Do' above stresses the children's request and is reflected in the reporting verb 'entreated')

5. A. "Never be a borrower," my father told me.
   B. My father advised me never to be a borrower.

FOR TEACHERS TO THINK ABOUT

1. Besides the above modes of reporting, imperatives can be reported in another way:
   1.   A. "Martin, open the window, "his father said.
      B. His father told Martin that he was to open the window.
   2. A. "Don't tease my pet dog, "she said to us.
      B. She told us that we were not to tease her pet dog.

However, the infinitive use as detailed earlier is to be preferred to the noun clause use. Why?

2. How can we explain the following reporting:
   A."Come here," my mother said to him
   B1. My mother asked him to go to her
   B2. My mother asked him to come to her.

SOME SPECIAL CASES OF REPORTING (for teachers' enrichment)

1. **The three types of conditionals** are reported as follows:

Eg: 1. If my brother comes early, we shall start the game.
        2. If my brother came early, we should start the game.
        3. If my brother had come, we should have started the game.

While reporting, No.1 changes to No.2, which changes to No.3

2. Reporting impersonal 'you'

We often say, "You cannot serve two masters at a time". Here, 'you' does not refer to any person i.e it is impersonal. In fact, it means 'one'. So, the reported form of that sentence is : My father told me that one could not serve two masters at a time.

3. Reporting exclamatory sentences

Study the following procedure:
1. A. "How naughty you are!"
   B. "You are very naughty."
   C. His mother said angrily that he was very naughty.

2. A. What a nice garden!"
   B. "It is indeed a very nice garden."
   C. She said admiringly that it was indeed a very nice garden.

4. Reporting incomplete sentences

Before reporting, incomplete sentences must be assumed complete, based on the context.
Eg: My teacher asked me, "When did you see your cousin?"
"Yesterday"
Reporting: My teacher asked me when I had seen my cousin. I replied that I had seen him/her the previous day.

In a nutshell

- If the reporting verbs(say, ask, told and so on) and the reported verbs (has, go/oes, knew/ had known and so on) should agree in tense – either present or past.
- Pronouns (I, you, we and so on)and adverbs (now, today, here and so on) showing nearness will become words of distance in reporting (he, she, they/ then, that day, there and so on). Likewise, present tense will shift to past tense and past tense to past perfect.
- While reporting questions, the verb-subject order changes to subject-verb order.
- Reported imperatives use 'to +verb'/ 'not to + verb' after 'that'.

Report the following sentences:
1. "Don't waste your time in watching these serials, "my uncle told me.
2. "Why didn't you come and talk to me in my chamber?" the Director asked me. I answered, "I didn't wish to disturb you as you seemed engaged, Sir."
3. "Didn't I tell you yesterday, Julie, about your brother's result?
   He has done miserably in the Annual Exams," the Principal said.

4. "Can I come with you to the club meeting this evening? I will feel lonely if I am to stay home, "Mrs. Emily told her husband.

5. "Do you know who is coming?" my sister asked him.

6. The doctor said to the boy," Did you take the syrup I had given you?"
The boy said," No, I don't like it. Do you think a medicine I don't like will do me good?"

7. "Listen to my speech, "said the lama to some students; and then write down what you think are the main points."

8. A student said to his teacher, "Shall I carry your luggage, Sir? It seems too heavy for you."

9. "Why don't you come up with the plain truth you say you have got from reliable sources? It appears now that you are just beating around the bush," the Principal told the School Captain.

10. "Have you written to your aunt to thank her for your birth day present?" my father said to my sister.

11. "If you have tears, prepare to shed them now, "Mark Antony told Romans.

12. "If I can catch him once upon the hip, I will feed fat the ancient grudge I bear him," Shylock said.

13. "If I live to be as old as Sibylla, I will die as chaste as Diana, "Portia said.

14. "I bear a charmed life, which must not yield to one of woman born," Macbeth said.

15. "Let your love be younger than yourself, or your affections cannot hold the bent," Duke Orsino said to a youth.

{**Answers:**

1. My uncle advised me not to waste my time in watching those serials.

2. The Director asked me why I hadn't come and spoken to him in his chamber. I answered that I had not wished to disturb him as he had seemed engaged.

3. The Principal asked Julie whether he hadn't told her the previous day about her brother's result. He had done miserably in the Annual exams.

4. Mrs. Emily asked her husband if she could go with him to the club meeting that evening. She added that she would feel lonely if she stayed home.

5. My sister asked him whether he knew who was coming.

6. The doctor asked the boy whether he had taken the syrup he had given. The boy informed the doctor that he had not because he didn't like it. The boy also asked the doctor if he thought a medicine he didn't like would do him good.

7. The lama advised some students to listen to his speech and then write down what they thought were the main points.

8. A student offered his help to his teacher, asking him whether he should carry his luggage. It seemed too heavy for the teacher.

9. The Principal asked the School Captain why he didn't come up with (or suggested to the captain to come up with) the plain truth he said he had got from reliable sources. He added that the Captain appeared then to be just beating around the bush.

10. My father asked his daughter whether she had written to her aunt to thank her for his daughter's birthday present.

11. Mark Antony told Romans to prepare to shed their tears if they had tears.

12. Shylock said that if he could catch him (Antonio) once upon the hip, he would feed fat the ancient grudge he bore him.

13. Portia said/vowed that if she lived to be as old as Sibylla, she would die as chaste as Diana.

14. Macbeth said that he bore a charmed life, which would not have to yield to one of woman born.

15. Duke Orsino told a youth that his love should be younger than himself, or his affections could not hold the bent.

----

8. LOGICAL CONNECTORS

Read the following story:

Once, a rich man wanted his only son to study in a reputed university, which was a little far away from his home town. *So,* he told his son, "My dear, there is no substitute for knowledge. *Therefore,* you go away from here in its pursuit and return a scholar. *In fact,* I am sad about your departure. *However,* I console myself because of the long-term benefit of such a short-term separation from you.

Thus, the son was away at the university and did very well as an exemplary scholar. *In other words,* he was rated 'outstanding' in academic as well as co-curricular fields. He was a good debater, an excellent singer and a leading marathoner, *for example.* *As a result,* the University faculty decided to award him 'the best scholar of the batch' medal.

However, all was not well back home. One day, he received the message that he should reach home soon, as his father was on his death-bed. The ailing man wanted to bequeath all his property to his son legally.

One of his mates, who resembled him in looks, heard about it and planned to cheat him. He dressed himself like the son and rushed to his house much ahead to claim the wealth. The father was about to hand over everything to him. *But* the real son reached there on time *so that* the lawyer was puzzled.

However, the lawyer decided to test both the boys. He asked them to shoot an arrow at the portrait of the father. *Whereas* the cheat readily shot at the portrait, the real son refused to do so. *Thus,* the property was handed over to the real son. The pretender, *consequently,* left the scene ashamed.

> **Note that the words underlined above make the narration smooth because they make the sentences inter-connected logically.**

First, study the following pieces of writing. Now let them think of any words or expressions that can occupy the gaps provided so that the reading becomes smooth.
1. This signature is not original;—, it is a forgery.
2. We still have another topic for discussion,—the decline of the standard of English

3. The treaty was ratified by almost all countries,—the EU.
4. Winter vacation can be made fruitful by doing so many things:—, you can enrich your English.
5. I wasn't disturbed by your interview;—I was looking forward to it.
6. What do you think? I didn't suggest the trip to Ukraine.—was I interested in it.—, it was he who suggested it.
7. You should—break up your ties with him—try to reform him.
8. In the northern parts, the temperature fall to—130 C—in the south it never goes below 90C.
9. —the poor struggle in the deserts of life, the rich dream in the gardens of life.
10. My father built in me the habit of early rising—it was not easy in the beginning.—, today, my body is well-timed to getting up at 4.30 AM every day.
11. All decisions were taken in due consultation with the students—they can be smoothly implemented.
12. I made a good fence around my farmhouse—our neighbourly warmth should strain any time in future.

(Possible answers: 1. In other words, 2.that is, 3. especially/for example 4. for instance, 5. In fact/ indeed/on the contrary, 6. Nor, in fact / 7. either . . . . or 8. whereas, 9. while 10. though; as a result, 11. so that, 12. lest.)

These logical connectors contribute to (a) smoothness and (b) coherence to our writing.

EXERCISES—1

Combine the following sentences, using suitable connectors such as: *No sooner . . . than, Whether . . . ,or , In other words, that is, especially, for example, for instance, indeed, on the contrary, Nor, in fact, either . . . . Or, whereas, while, though, as a result, so that, lest. not only . . . but also*

1. I don't mind meeting you in New York Y. Los Angeles also will do.
2. I shall buy mutton. I shall buy chicken if that is available.
3. Richard does not eat maize. I don't either.
4. My tired son lay in bed. Immediately he fell asleep.
5. Teachers and elders inculcate good values in the kids. Patriotism is such a value.
6. Is she telling the truth? I don't know that.
7. Perseverance helps one in hard times. Perseverance is one's ability to hold on and on.
8. Breathing gives out CO2. But photosynthesis takes in the same gas.
9. Use your time properly. If not, you will regret later.
10. Environmental protection is dear to all countries. Bhutan is an example.

{Possible answers: 1. I don't mind meeting you either in Sudan or in Los Angelus. 2. I shall buy either mutton or chicken, depending on the availability. 3. Neither Richard nor I eat maize. 4. No sooner did my tired son lie in bed than he fell asleep. 5. Teachers and elders inculcate in kids good values, patriotism for example. 6. I don't know whether she is telling the truth. 7. Perseverance, that is one's ability to hold on and on, helps one in hard times. 8. Whereas breathing gives out CO2, photosynthesis takes in the same gas. 9. Use your time properly or you will regret later. 10. 10. Environmental protection is dear to all countries, especially Bhutan.}

EXERCISES—2

Fill in the blanks with appropriate connectors:

1. I think this is a different issue,—the racial discrimination in S. Africa.
2. The whole school,—the principal, congratulated the football team.
3. The literary Club can do so many things:—, it can publish a magazine.
4. My mother was not very happy about the new business;—she was very apprehensive of the risks involved.
5. My sister did not want to marry him—she was I interested in him.—, she did not like his short temper.
6. You should—love your profession—quit it soon.
7. Edward is clever and hard working—her brother, Kate is lazy and careless.
8. —robbers and dacoits don't respect people's lives, the police protects them.
9. I hated Mathematics—I always tried to master the subject.
10. We are not in the right place;—we are elsewhere.

(Possible answers: 1. that is, 2. especially/for example 3. for instance, 4. In fact/indeed/on the contrary, 5 though, in fact 6. either . . . . or 7. whereas 8. while 9. though 10. in other words)

9. PUNCTUATION

Read the following story and carefully note the use of the punctuation marks used in it:

"Hang him not, set him free," read the judge's hand-written verdict sheet. The clerks in the court of law would type them – that was the practice. The clerk on duty, therefore, typed it and the accused was hanged!! Why? The typed version read, "Hang him, not set him free." Look! The life of the man depended just on the comma – the position of the comma, precisely.

The accused was charge-sheeted because a blood-stained knife had been discovered in his traveling bag. In fact, the murderer was another person – a co-traveller of the accused—, who, after stabbing and killing the victim, had laid the blood-dripping knife in the bag of the accused. Caught thus apparently red-handed, this man was tried in the court, and the court acquitted him, realizing his innocence.

The judiciary believed in the dictum: 'The innocent should not be punished even if a thousand criminals escape.' Here, the innocent man escaped. So did the criminal. For, the latter was not traced by the police.

A. Exclamation mark (!)

It is used to express strong emotions. So it is common after an interjection (Alas! Heavens! My God! etc.) and exclamatory sentences such as:
> How I hate him!
> You little rogue!
> What a terrible storm!
It is also used for abrupt, peremptory orders:
> Get out! I can't tolerate this insult.
> Quiet! What a nonsense!

B. Colons. (:)

They are used to introduce (a) a direct speech (b) a list of items and (c) an explanation or a suggestion.

Eg: 1.Shakespeare said: "The apparel proclaims the man."

2. To me, the difficult authors are: Sir Walter Scott, James Joyce, T.S. Eliot and Salmon Rushdie.
3. The gist of what he says is this: he is determined to get what he deserves.

C. Commas (,)

in inverted commas: to

1. set the direct speech off from the rest of the sentence:
    Tom said, "The house that I like is for sale."
    "The house that I like," Tom said, "is for sale."

(**Note:** Single quotation marks are used inside the double marks when a quotation exists within another quotation:
"I heard Edward say, 'Be careful,' before the plank fell, 'said Kate.)

Quotation marks or italics are used to set off words that are referred to as words and are not a part of the basic sentence structure.

When you use the word 'clever', use it carefully.

2. to separate off appositional phrases and clauses:

    ✓ Lord Buddha, who taught us ahimsa, was a great man.
    ✓ Asoka, having conquered Kalinga, decided to stop all wars.
    ✓ The police, however, failed in its attempt.
    ✓ She has, to my surprise, picked up the skill fast.
    ✓ The Arabs, who were trained by the British, did well.

D. Brackets ( )

Generally, two brackets, two dashes and two commas are used to introduce extra information or classification. This is called parenthesis.
(A single dash shows an interruption in the flow of thought.)

Examples:
*   The speaker (the poet himself) reveals his dilemma through his speeches. (We can replace the brackets with a pair of dashes or commas)
*   My elder sister—nobody knows where she is gone—was very kind to me.

A. Semi colons (;)

1. Two simple sentences can be combined with the help of a co-ordinating conjunction, before which we use a semi colon. Sometimes, only the semi colon is used, dropping the conjunction.
*   Her favourite serial is 'Woman'; consequently, she watches it daily.
*   Travelling can be a pleasing experience; however, it can be stressful for a large family.
*   We enjoyed going to the ocean; the children collected shells.
*   We laughed; we cried; we shared memories.

2. Semicolons are used to separate sentences which are closely related in thought, where a full stop would be too complete a stop.

- As Caesar loved me, I weep for him; as he was fortunate, I rejoice at it; as he was valiant, I honour him.
- Reading maketh a full man; conference a ready man; writing an exact man.

Exercise.

Use all the punctuation marks you think are needed in the following:
1. perhaps said he there may be such monsters as you describe
2. what on earth he asked me do you mean
3. these suits have just arrived he said would you like one
4. yes id like one she replied but how about the price
5. only Rs 400 each said he goodness that's too much she replied I wont pay more than Rs 300 for one
6. he is engaged to me I said is he since when since yesterday well congratulations has your father consented he said
7. pearl buck got the nobel prize for her good earth
8. James who is a fat boy said I have ten slices of bread a couple of eggs for breakfast
9. my mother said to my father would you come to the kitchen for a help
10. sir pleaded the boy I m only asking you to help me to find some work I m not a beggar and so please don't treat me like one
11. do you know shouted the customer to the shopkeeper that adulteration is a crime and that I plan to send the butter I bought from you to the authorities
12. I know said the child that great author homer wrote the iliad
13. I said can I see the manager certainly said the accountant
14. You are a stupid boy shouted the angry father do you think that I aam going to send you to school any longer
15. Matthew said to Kate will it be possible for you to come to my house on sunday ill explain some of the problems to you.
16. there was once a poor man who could no longer keep his only son the son said dear father things are so bad that I feel I am a burden to you id rather go forth and seek some way of earning my bread his father gave him his blessing and said what a terrible thing it is to part from you ill always pray for your happiness.

{Answers:
1. "Perhaps," said he, "there may be such monsters as you describe."
2. "What on earth," he asked me, "do you mean?"
3. "These suits have just arrived," he said. "Would you like one?"
4. "Yes, I'd like one," she replied," but how about the price?"
5. "Only Rs.400/—each," said he. "Goodness! That's too much," she replied. "I won't pay more than Rs.300/—for one."
6. "He is engaged to me," I said.
   " Is he? Since when?"
   "Since yesterday."
   "Well! Congratulations. Has your father consented?" he said.

7. Pearl Buck got the Nobel Prize for her Good Earth.

8. James, who is a fat boy, said, "I have ten slices of bread, a couple of eggs for breakfast."

9. My mother said to my father, "Would you come to the kitchen for a help?"

10. "Sir," pleaded the boy. "I am only asking you to help me to find some work. I'm not a beggar and so please don't treat me like one. "

11. "Do you know," shouted the customer to the shopkeeper," that adulteration is a crime and that I plan to send the butter I bought from you to the authorities?"

12. "I know," said the child, "that the great author, Homer wrote the Iliad."

13. I said, "Can I see the manager?" "Certainly," said the accountant.

14. "You are a stupid boy," shouted the angry father."Do you think that I am going to send you to school any longer?"

15. Matthew said to Kate, "Will it be possible for you to come to my house on Sunday? I'll explain some of the problems to you."

16. There was once a poor man, who could no longer keep his only son. The son said, "Dear father, things are so bad that I feel I am a burden to you. I'd rather go forth and seek some way of earning my bread."

    His father gave him his blessing and said, "What a terrible thing it is to part from you! I'll always pray for your happiness."}

10. PHRASAL VERBS

Take note of the phrasal verbs (underlined) used in the story below:

Kate is average at studies. Though she worked hard, something obstructed her from scoring high. It got her down. One day, while doing a Project Work in History, Kate was stuck up half way. Though she laboured at it, she was not able to progress. Besides, she was afraid of not submitting the PW on time. So, she called on her friend, Michael, got his PW and copied a part of it though unwillingly.

Laura, an intelligent and hard working class mate of Kate's, came to know about the PW copying. And, she knew that Kate was going to get high marks because of Michael's brilliant work. Laura, who believed in hard work, too would score high. However, someone's scoring good marks without actually sweating for it disturbed her. She just could not put up with someone's undeserved scoring. She reported the matter to the History teacher, who she thought would not let her off for copying. As expected, the teacher awarded zero to Kate.

The next day, when it was raining, Kate ran against Laura in the town without an umbrella. It was getting late for the school. Kate saw through Laura's misery. She called Laura in and they went to school together under the same umbrella.

The contexts tell the meaning of the phrasal verbs underlined as:

Got her down   = made her sad
Laboured at   = worked hard at
Called on   = visited (a person)
Put up with   = tolerate
Let her off   = excuse her
Ran against   = met by chance
Saw through   = detected

Phrasal verbs are a combination of 'verb + preposition' or 'verb + adverb'. The preposition or the adverb added to the verb—named '*particle*'—makes a big difference in the meaning of the root verb. For example, 'call at' means 'visit a place' whereas 'call for' means 'demand' and so on.

The following examples show the variety of meaning-possibilities phrasal verbs:

1. **Accommodate sb/sth to** = adapt or change according to
Why not accommodate yourself to the new policies?
I can accommodate my food habits to vegetarianism.
2. **Accommodate sb with sth** = grant or supply
My father accommodated me with an added amount of pocket money.
The Youth Division is ready accommodate volunteers with a loan for counseling activities.
3. **Accompanied by** = gone as a companion
The minister was accompanied by his secretary.
4. **Accompanied with** = occur along with
Often, heavy monsoons are accompanied with massive landslides.
5. **Act from** = act out of or because of
After the accident, the child stammered; she was acting from fear
6. **Act on/upon** = act according to/ based on
The police got a tip-off and acted on that information.
7. **Act up** = give pain or irritation owing to malfunction
Good Heavens! The car is acting up again
8. **Adapted for** = modified so as to suit
The novel is adapted for a stage show.
9. **Adapted from** = adapted from an original
This one-act play is adapted from a Greek tragedy.
10. **Adapted to** = changed according to
After coming to the monastery, his mind is adapted to the stillness of the surroundings.
11. **Agree with/ to/ (up)on** = with sb/ to sb's opinion/ upon a plan of action
Later Mathematicians agreed with Pythagoras
It was so difficult to agree to the Principal's suggestion.
The cabinet agreed on a detailed campaign against smoking.
12. **Alive with** = full of the liveliness of
A college campus is alive with shouts and laughs of youngsters.
13. **Alive to** = be sensitive to/be fully aware of
A seasoned businessman, he is alive to the risks in transactions.
14. **Back away** = move back hesitantly
As it came near the fence, the cow backed away.
15. **Back off** = give up a claim to
The miscreants had claimed that the abandoned car was theirs; but they backed off at the sight of the police.
16. **Back out** = withdraw
My father was banking on my uncle's help. But the latter backed out at the last moment.
17. **Back up** = support
The US backs up India's Rsclear non-proliferation efforts.
18. Bear down = overcome
Constant efforts can bear down the initial difficulties in Maths calculations.
19. **Bear on/upon** =be relevant to
The theme of environment protection in the poem bears on the government policy of GNH.
20. **Bear out** = prove or confirm
The present-day global warming bears out H. G Wells' predictions in his writings.
21. **Bear up** = face and endure

Abraham Lincoln is said to have <u>borne up</u> well in life despite a chain of setbacks.

22. Blow over = disappear (from memory)

Today, the corruption news you shared is an issue; but in a year it will <u>blow over</u>.

23. Blow up = explode and destroy

Nobody suspected that the anti-social elements would <u>blow up</u> the school building.

24. Break away = secede; give up (a habit)

India is trying hard to stop some states' attempts to <u>break away</u> from the main land.

25. Break into = force/ burst into

It was expected that the burglar would <u>break into</u> the bungalow.

Unexpectedly, my sister broke into tears.

26. Break off = pause/ choke while speaking

Though angry, he tried to control himself but <u>broke off</u> in the middle and walked away,

27. Break up = go into pieces/end an alliance/disperse

In the scorching heat, the boulders were <u>breaking up</u>.

I smell signs of my nephew's romance <u>breaking up</u>.

The strikers were very big in number and it was hard for the police to break up the mob.

28. Carry off = win/ succeed despite difficulties.

Master Darren <u>carried off</u> all the first prizes on the Sports day.

29. Carry out = perform/ fulfil

When it comes to <u>carrying out</u> her duties, my sister is outstanding civil servant.

30. Carry on (with) = manage (continue to manage)

It is pretty difficult to <u>carry on</u> my LLB practice amid frequent disturbance.

You had better carry on with the construction work even when I am away.

31. Come about = happen

It so <u>came about</u> that our enemies proved stronger than we expected.

32. Come across = meet/ find by chance

Yesterday, my mother <u>came across</u> an old religious relic inside the wardrobe.

33. Come apart = come to pieces

My son was so sad that in minutes after buying it, the toy plane <u>came apart</u>.

34. Come between = interfere in a relationship.

It is not advisable to <u>come between</u> the bickering spouses. Leave them alone.

35. Come by = get with difficulty

In this competitive world, a gainful job is hard to <u>come by</u>.

36. Come through = recover/ escape an injury

It took almost a month for my ailing father to <u>come through</u>.

Thank God! You <u>came through</u> the dangerous landslide.

37. Consist in = be the only or main part in

Good manners <u>consist</u> not only in respect for others.

38. Consist of = comprise/ be made of

Our activities <u>consist of</u> organizing sports besides mobilizing fund for them.

39. Cut down (on) = reduce the use of

Thank God! My mom decided to <u>cut down</u> (on) smoking.

40. Cut in/into = interrupt (a conversation/talk)

It's not good manners to <u>cut in</u> while others speak.

41. Cut out for = have the qualities to become

Nicholas is <u>cut out for</u> an architect. / The couple are cut out for each other.

42. **Die away** = lose strength

By dusk, the brightness of the torch <u>dies away</u> as the cells exhaust by time.

43. **Die down** = grow less aggressive and less loud.

The assaulted prisoner screamed aloud but soon his screams <u>died down</u>.

44. **Die off** = die one after another. It's off season; the fruits <u>die off</u>.

45. **Die out** = become extinct. The dinosaurs had <u>died out</u> long ago.

46. **Distinguish between** = discriminate.

Our new boss does not <u>distinguish between</u> seniors and Juniors.

47. **Distinguish by** = identify with the help of.

The captain can be <u>distinguished by</u> his stammering.

48. **Distinguished for** = be known for. Dr. Raj is <u>distinguished for</u> his statesmanship.

49. **Distinguish from** = know the difference between

A well-educated person <u>distinguishes</u> talent <u>from</u> show.

50. **Do away with**=remove/ abolish. Some think that we should <u>do away with</u> examinations

51. **Do down** = disparage/criticize.

In Indian democracy, the opposition will always <u>do down</u> the ruling party's policies.

52. **Done for** = ruined/ destroyed. His strict father caught him smoking; now he is <u>done for</u>.

53. **Done in/ up** = exhausted. She was <u>done in</u> after three matches of basket ball.

54. **Do up** = fasten/ make oneself look better

The girl <u>does up</u> her hair before the mirror.

She takes an hour at least to do herself up.

55. **Eat away** = destroy by taking away parts of

Strong winds <u>eat away</u> the top soil from the hill.

56. **Eat into** = dissolve parts of. Strong acids <u>eat into</u> the walls of their containers.

57. **Expect from** = thinking to receive from

The Principal <u>expects</u> full co-operation <u>from</u> her subordinates.

58. **Expect of** = thinking that others will possess.

High-level dedication is <u>expected of</u> the students of this school.

59. **Fall in with** = meet with/ agree to.

I was so glad that I fell in with Kate after our school days.

At last, my boss <u>falls in with</u> my suggestions for improvement.

60. **Fall for** = yield/ be attracted to. Yangzom readily <u>fell for</u> his looks.

61. **Fall through** = flop. If not properly planned, your project will <u>fall through</u>.

62. **Fall out** = happen/ drop out.

If you trick the thieves, all will fall out according to our designs.

We should discuss seriously why so many student <u>fall out</u> every year from their studies.

63. **Fall out with** = quarrel. Unfortunately, my nephew <u>fell out with</u> his father .

64. **Get sth across to sb** = make sb understand sth.

Poor teachers cannot <u>get</u> real messages <u>across to</u> his/her pupils.

65. **Get along** = manage/ succeed. It is great that you <u>get along</u> even in hard times.

66. **Get at sth**. = discover and reveal. Their investigation will surely <u>get at the</u> facts.

67. **Get away/ with** = escape/ escape from being caught.

The newcomer came to the meeting hall and <u>got away</u> unnoticed.

Mr. X was an accomplice in the burglary; but he got away with the burglary.

68. **Get over sth** = Emily tried her best; however, she was unable to <u>get over</u> her laziness.

69. **Get round sb** = persuade. At last, she was able to <u>get round</u> her father to let her go.

70. **Get through** = reach/ pass the exam.

Though I didn't expect it, my words got through to my brother.

He says that the ICSE is easier to <u>get through</u> than the CBSE.

71. **Hang about** = loiter. The Police notice a man <u>hang about</u> the town.

72. **Hang back** = hesitate. The cat came near a puddle and <u>hung back</u>.

73. **Hang together** = be united / be consistent.

Operation Blackboard is our ambitious project; let's <u>hang together</u> in its execution.

Please edit your recommendations; many of them don't <u>hang together</u>.

74. **Hold off** = stay/ delay/ keep at a distance

As usual there will be wind, which will not <u>hold off</u> before 5.00 PM.

75. **Hold on** = be firm. The team lost in the first half; still it decided to <u>hold on</u>.

76. **Hold out** = keep resisting.

The Tamil Tigers <u>held out</u> for ten years despite govt. pressure

77. **Hold over** = postpone. We will have to <u>hold over</u> the match till next week.

78. **Hold up** = delay. The agitators <u>held up</u> air services for three hours.

79. **Influence (up) on** = have an effect on. Movie fashions have an <u>influence on</u> youngsters.

80. **Influence with** = (a person). For my son's admission, I shall use your <u>influence with</u> the college management.

81. **Involve in** = be a part of/ be caught in. Martin was found <u>involved in</u> the dispute.

82. **Involve with** = closely linked with. Dear son, don't be <u>involved with</u> the miscreants.

83. **Jump at** = accept readily. Mr. Nicholas <u>jumped at</u> the opportunity to abuse his cousin.

84. **Jump for joy.** My daughter <u>jumped for joy</u> at the news of her pass in the exams.

85. **Knock about** = lead a nomadic life.

Enough is enough; Mr. Andrew decided to stop <u>knocking about</u>.

86. **Knock off** = stop work; compose in a hurry.

My friends aren't here; they have <u>knocked off</u> for tea.

In fact, I had no time. But as my House captains asked me, I knocked off a short story.

87. **Lay down** = establish. The daily wages are already <u>laid down</u> by the government.

88. **Lay/put by** = save for future. The ants always <u>lay by</u> food for the winter months.

89. **Lay off** = discontinue work. The labourers declared to <u>lay off</u> for a fortnight.

90. **Lay out** = design. A foreign architect is called in to <u>lay out</u> the city.

91. **Look in** = make a brief visit.

On his return home from the US, he will look in on his uncle's.

92. **Look into** = examine. The SP said that they were <u>looking into</u> the murder case.

93. **Look upon as** = regard as. The minister is <u>looked upon as</u> a role model by the youth.

94. **Make after sb.** = pursue. The sniffer dog <u>makes after</u> the thief.

95. **Make away with** = steal and run away. The burglar <u>made away with</u> the statue.

96. **Make for** = <u>move towards</u>/contribute to.

The culprit was found making for the monastery.

Regular reading will definitely make for breadth of vision.

97. **Put sb. forward** = nominate sb. as

They <u>put</u> Peter <u>forward</u> as the school councilor.

98. **Put sb. off** = avoid him/her with excuses.

These reasons are not enough; I know you are <u>putting</u> me <u>off</u>.

99. **Rest on** = depend on. His fame <u>rests on</u> the depth in his writings.

100. **Rest with** = vested with/ belong to.

You cannot issue the warrant; that power <u>rests with</u> the Commissioner.

101. **Result from** = happen as a result of

A lot of confusion <u>results from</u> vague explanations and ill-defined leadership

102. **Result in** = the outcome of sth. Unplanned work <u>result in</u> lack-lustre performance.

103. **See to sth**. = ensure that it is done. Peter, <u>see to</u> the proper safety of the guests.

104. **See through** = detect what is hidden.

The clever lion <u>saw through</u> the evil designs of the wolf.

105. **Set aside** = ignore/ keep aside

The hostile countries should <u>set aside</u> their differences and sit for discussions.

Let's set aside some funds for helping the needy.

106. **Set in** = start. This time, winter <u>set in</u> a little early.

107. **Tell apart** = distinguish. You need sharpness in order to <u>tell between</u> the twin projects

108. **Tell sb. off**= scold by pointing out sb's mistakes.

I would <u>tell</u> my sister <u>off</u> and make her aware of her mistakes.

109. **Turn down** = refuse. The Secretary <u>turned down</u> his application for transfer.

110. **Turn out to be** = proved to be in the end

All her pretensions to be wise <u>turned out to be</u> hollow at last.

111. **Turn over** = change. The drug addict recently turned over a new leaf.

112. **Turn over** = do the business at the rate of

The firm recently <u>turns over</u> Rs. 20, 0000/—per week.

113. **Vex at** = annoy. They are <u>vexed at</u> the unstable power supply.

114. **Vex with** = The public get <u>vexed with</u> a week-long strike.

115. **Win over** = persuade. At last I was able to <u>win over</u> my unwilling friend.

116. **Win against** = be victorious against. The Germans <u>won against</u> the Dutch.

117. **Weigh up** = assess. Isn't it necessary to <u>weigh up</u> the need study for the reform?

118. **Weigh with** = influence. My sad story hardly <u>weighed with</u> my listeners.

119. **Work off** = remove. It may be difficult to <u>work off</u> your bad image among the public.

120. **Work on/up** = excite/ arouse

My friend's hardships in life should <u>work on</u> human hearts.

A charismatic leader can work up the passion of the staff.

Exercises:

Supply the correct particle in the gaps so as to make the sentences meaningful:

1. After a long discussion, they agreed—a plan of action.
2. However I try, I cannot agree—his suggestion.
3. When did you complain—the District administration?
4. I decided to complain—improper sanitation facilities in the house.
5. Sir Bedivere found it difficult to part—Excalibur.
6. It is true that my son cannot part—his friends.
7. In that lonely desert, he listened—bird songs.
8. We listened keenly—the lama's lecture.
9. The success in your life is a result—planned work.
10. Lack of co-operation can result—a bad work ethos

{Answers:
1. On/upon
2. to
3. to
4. Of/ about
5. with
6. from
7. for
8. to
9. of
10. in }

11. REMEDIAL ENGLISH

It is natural that students reach good proficiency in English through a series of tumbles, shocks and knocks – errors. Good students seek the elders' and teachers' help to overcome these initial difficulties and achieve a fair command over the language.

Many teachers are confronted with the problem of their students' errors especially in their written work. Often, students face, inter alia, the following problems:

1. Fragment (F)
2. Run-on sentences (RO)
3. 'S'-ending(including 'concord')
4. -ed ending.
5. Wrong use of the apostrophe
6. Pronoun confusion.
7. Tense shift.
8. Misspelling
9. Inappropriate vocabulary.

1. Fragments. (F)

Ask the students to see whether the following sentences are incomplete (F) or Complete sentences (C). Let them use these letters (F&C) to mark these sentences. This is a diagnostic test.

1. The droning of the plane makes it hard for me to hear.	(C)
2. However, the matter forgotten altogether.	(F)
3. They been living here since 1998.	(F)
4. You made me confused because of a lot of reasoning.	(C)
5. Beating around the bush and not coming to the point.	(F)
6. With this evidence and having no will.	(F)
7. The river beyond the hill and beside the river.	(F)
8. I think you'd score high, going at this pace.	(C)
9. Thinking positively itself can be healthy.	(C)
10. One of the most pressing needs of the time.	(F)
11. To see things as they are is not easy.	(C)
12. Tired and disgusted because of much work.	(F)
13. Determined to achieve as you go ahead.	(F)

14. There is no use criticising things as they are. (C)
15. Whenever he is hungry, making himself some fast food. (F)
16. If I reach there in time for dinner (F)
17. If she dances well, so can I. (C)
18. The article was incoherent though written legibly. (C)
19. Since I came here early enough (F)
20. He who climbs too high in life. (F)

When examined carefully, Fragments Nos.2, 3 contain incomplete verbs. Nos. 6, 7 are incomplete with prepositional phrases. Nos. 5, 12, 13, 15 are incomplete with verb phrases. Nos. 16, 19, 20 have incomplete subordinate clauses and No. 10 is a fragment as it is a noun phrase.

Now, the teacher, having understood the exact nature of his students' Fragments, can show them how to make them complete. For example, No.2 can be rectified as:

However, the matter was forgotten altogether.

2. Run-on sentences. (RO)

This defect is in one way the opposite of the 'fragment'. Let us consider the causes of the RO.

1. My boss has an idea that we should consider, it might solve our problem. (Here, the first sentence should have stopped at the comma. (This is called comma splice.) This error can be rectified as:
My boss has an idea that we must consider. It might solve our problem.

2. Emma had better hurry she's sure to be late. (One way of correcting the RO here is to use a coordinating conjunction-and, but, or/nor, for, so etc.) with a comma just in front of it, or just a semicolon instead of the conjunction.

Example: Emma had better hurry, or she is sure to be late.

The RO sentence, "Matthew likes pork curry chicken chilly is also fine with him" can be corrected as:

"Matthew likes pork curry; chicken chilly is also . . . ."

Another way to remedy the RO is shown below:

The nearest town to our house is Tokyo, it is 42miles away.

Here, we can just subordinate one of the RO sentences like:

- The nearest town to our house is Tokyo, it is 42miles away.
- The nearest town to our house is Tokyo though it is 42miles away.

There is still another way: ie. by reducing one of these sentences into a participial phrase like:

- RO : You will love to stay with Joseph he is so lovely.
- Correction: You will love to stay with lovely Joseph.

3. 's'-ending

Our students get confused by the final's' of the following categories:
  i.   regular plural nouns.
  ii. singular verbs that agree with the third person singular subjects in simple present.
  iii. 's' ending in the primary auxiliaries: is, was, has does. Of these No.2 above has been found the most acute even among the advanced learners.

Exercises and drills of the following nature can rectify this error:

Rewrite the following sentences into those with plural subjects:

1. A rolling stone gathers no moss.
2. A stitch in time saves nine.
3. That old saying is driving me up the wall.
4. This sentence is changing its tone now.
5. Jo's brother has given up the idea.
6. The neighbour has prayed for long.
7. Does the complaint matter much?
8. His brother doesn't care a bit.

4. The—ed ending.

In correct language use, the—ed ending is used as the:

1. Simple past of a regular verb.
2. Past participle of a regular verb in perfect tense.
3. Past participle of a regular verb in passive voice.
4. Past participle of a regular verb as an adjective.
5. Perfect infinitive and passive infinitive.

All others are errors. Correction and mastery drills comprise:

i.   Changing of all simple present tense into simple past in a group of sentences.
ii. (For example) Recall what happened on your last birthday. Use simple past and write about 5 sentences starting : On my last birthday . . .
iii. (For example)

A. Hannah baited the hook
B. Did . . . .?
C. Hannah didn't . . . .

I. Think of different situations in which the following expressions can be used and then make sentences, using them:
-recorded marks
-assigned task
-finished projects
-rat-eaten butter
-torn pants

5. Wrong use of the apostrophe.

Students should be aware that an apostrophe is used also to indicate omission such as:

It's = it is
Won't = will not
Isn't = is not

6. Tense shift.

This is a common problem with our students, rather, with our teachers. Inconsistent tense use by teachers in spoken English is imbibed by students. Children are like wet cement. Most things that fall on it leave an impression.

The following are a few guidelines, combining both the methods to tackle 6 and 7:
A. A piece of writing needs a time framework based on a dominant tense.

Ask the students to recast all the s. present tense uses into s. past in the following paragraph:

Leena takes promises very seriously. She never forgives any one for breaking one. In addition, she considers the slightest little agreement to be a full-fledged promise. So people often find Leena counting on them to do things they have no intention of doing. She fills her life with trumped-up promises and then makes a huge fuse when most of those promises fall through

B. Shifting pronouns without a good reason distracts a reader.

Pronoun confusion	Correction
1. When people watch silly or violent programmes, they try to imitate the end up making a fool of yourself.	When people watch . . . . actors and they . . . . . making fools actors and you of themselves.

In this way, pronouns can be corrected.

9. Misspelling

Ask students to keep a spelling book or a page in their exercise books. Let them read every word that they have entered as having difficult spelling. Again, let them read and NOT SPELL daily at least once. 'Spelling is most often caught rather than taught.'

10. Inappropriate Vocabulary.

This is a vexing problem. In fact, one cannot suggest an easy remedy to this problem. However, a positive thing is that many of our students use new words in their language. Whether they use them correctly, or not is, of course, an important matter. But the fondness for new words in itself is a sign of adolescence and growth. Here, the role of the teacher is that of a patient guide. After all, your students have dared. We must urge our students to use the Oxford Dictionary (or any other standard one) for correct usage of words.

12. A MODEL GRAMMAR QUIZ

1. In the sentence, 'The plan itself is good 'itself' is an emphatic pronoun/reflexive pronoun?

   Emphatic

2. 'It was a blinding lightning'
   There are two '-ings, which is the participle which the noun?
   Blinding-participle, lightning-noun

3. What is the Past Participle of 'grind'

   Ground

4. Simple Present form of 'lain'?

   Lie

5. The news is—(broadcast) in the BBS-Use the right word.

   Broadcast

6. What is the Latin word from which 'Tense' is derived?

   Tempus

7. What is the Past Participle of 'thrust'

   Thrust

8. Which is the acceptable plural: Sons-in-law/Son-in-laws

   Sons-in-law

9. All spoke well of the Principal. Which part of speech is 'All'

   Pronoun

10. Each of the participants (has/have) been given a file. Which one is correct-has or have?
    has

11. 'Later' refers to time. What does 'latter' refer to?

    Position

12. I had a letter from my brother,—? What is the correct question tag?

    Didn't I?

13. "Sorry I could not come before.' What part of speech is before
    adverb

14. It was a lonely place, well chosen. Pick out the adverb.

    Well

15. He sounded—(rough) but friendly—Use the correct form of the word in bracket.
    rough

16. They made him the captain. Pick out the complement.

    Captain

17. A lot of time (have/has) been wasted. Use the correct word from the brackets.
    has

Correct after diagnosis.

18. Having finished his HW, his mother gave Kate food

    Having finished his Homework, Kate was given food by his mother. (Diagnosis: the subject of the participial phrase doesn't agree with that of the sentence)

19. A lot of water has flown down the river

    Flowed (diagnosis: Past participle of 'flow' is flowed')

20. I have met her last week

    I met her (Diagnosis: 'Last week' indicates definite past time but Present Perfect is indefinite in its past time reference)

21. Matthew is the eldest of the two daughters.

    Elder (Diagnosis: There are only two and it refers to family members)

22. The more he advised me, the lesser I obeyed him

    'the less' (Diagnosis: 'Less' is already a comparative; so no need of 'lesser')

23. A lot of damages were caused by the flood

    'damage was' (Diagnosis: 'damages' in the plural means compensation)

24. If I were a bird, I'd have flown to safety.

    Diagnosis: This is an imaginary condition in the present. So the main clause should be 'I'd fly to safety'

25. News travel fast

    'News' is always singular. So it should be 'News travels fast')

26. Perhaps she may come
    ('Perhaps' and 'may' mean the same. So either is redundant) So, 'She may come' or 'Perhaps she will come'

Distinguish

30. *Kate, our captain leads the team.*
    The speaker calls Kate and speaks to him

    Kate, our captain, leads the team.
    Kate is the team captain.

31. *I needn't have bought the pen.* (I bought) and so I regret it

    He did not need to buy the pen. (didn't buy) because it wasn't necessary

32. *He shouts as if he is mad.* (The speaker is unsure whether he is mad or not)

    He shouts as if he were mad. (not mad in fact; but he shouts like a mad man.)

33. *He stopped talking.* (He is silent now)

    He stopped to talk. (He halted (he was moving) in order to talk)

34. *He teaches her better than I.* (He and I teach her. He is a better teacher)

    He teaches her better than me. (He teaches both her and me. Somehow, he teaches her better.)

35. *She has published her novel late.* (Somehow she was late)

She has published her novel lately. (She published it recently.)

36. Give the Passive of:

    Who are you referring to?

    Who is/are being referred to by you?

37. Change into Past tense:

    It costs you nothing even if you lie still in bed.

    It cost you nothing even if you lay still in bed.

38. "Did you run fast yesterday, Edward?" his mother asked him . . . . Report.

    His mother asked Edward whether he/she had run fast the previous day.

QUESTION BANK

For Class IX – XII

I. A

Complete sentence B as similar in meaning as possible to sentence A:

1. A. "Are you happy with this amount today?" he asked me
   B. He asked me whether . . .
2. A. He stopped the vehicle as soon as he saw the police.
   B. Scarcely . . .
3. A. The box is too heavy to be lifted.
   B. The box is so . . .
4. A. He rushed to his son when Michael saw him.
   B. On . . .
5. A. Most of the towns in Bhutan are not as big as Los Angeles.
   B. . . . biggest . . .
6. A. Who was offering you the pen?
   B. . . . by whom?
7. A. I don't know why you are disappointed.
   B. . . . . .your disappointment.
8. A. Everyone knows the composer of this music.
   B. . . . composed this music.
9. A. He is so stubborn that he cannot yield to that temptation.
   B. He is too . . .
10. A. The fact that you are lazy proves this.
    B. Your . . .

I B

Supply the right words in the blanks:

1. His wife is disgusted—him for his alcoholic addiction
2. His parents' arrival relieved him—fear
3. This paddy field abounds—mice.
4. Then Kuwait appealed—the UNO for intervention.
5. He is popular; but he is wanting—sympathy.
6. She was accused immediately—theft.
7. He is unsteady; we cannot rely—him.
8. As he was sick, his parents sent—a lama.
9. It suddenly occurred—him that he should go abroad.
10. Our games teacher is so keen—our continuing the practice.

II A

Complete sentence B as similar in meaning as possible to sentence A:

1. A. Of all the countries of the world, Vatican is the smallest.
   B. . . . small . . .
2. A. Long years of sufferings had given her patience.
   B. She . . .
3. A. She is not as calm as his sister.
   B. . . . . calmer . . .
4. A. Can you tell me when he will be tried?
   B. . . . trial?
5. A. His action seldom smells of corruption.
   B. . . . by his action.
6. A. As soon as my car comes, my pet dog barks.
   B. No sooner . . .
7. A. The public laughed at the desire of the dying man.
   B. . . . by the public.
8. A. It was much discussed that our economy is worsening.
   B. . . . . was much discussed.
9. A. Mark Antony praised Caesar for his valour.
   B. . . . by Mark Antony.
10. A. My uncle told Benjamin, "If you were older, I would not forgive you."
    B. My uncle told Benjamin that . . .

II B

Supply the right word in the gaps:

1. The Manager could not agree—our suggestion.
2. We should avail ourselves—this opportunity.
3. The plane bound—Delhi had to crash-land.
4. Our discussion must be confined—the main topic.
5. The judge's partiality deprived him—first position.
6. Our boss will never forgive you if you are forgetful—your duty.
7. Our teacher insists—rewriting the answer.
8. Some rich men look down down—the poor.
9. Somehow, he passes—for a learned man.
10. Lady Diana was worthy—the respect of all people.

III A

1. A. He burst out in tears when he heard the news.
   B. On . . .
2. A. I did not know why he was angry.
   B. . . . anger.
3. A. Please tell me when he will arrive.
   B. . . . arrival.
4. A. All know the author of this novel.
   B. . . . who . . .
5. A. Who was teaching you grammar?
   B. . . . . by whom?
6. A. The audience loudly cheered the Mayor's speech.
   B. . . . by the audience.
7. A. Circumstances have given her enough courage.
   B. She . . .
8. A. Brutus accused Caesar of ambition.
   B. . . . by Brutus.
9. A. You have never heard of a happy millionaire.
   B. . . . been heard..
10. A. He made objections as soon as he came.
    B. No sooner . . .

III B

Supply the right word in the gaps:
1. With the exception—none, all our friends were present.
2. Can there be an exception—the fact that we all are mortals?
3. I am afraid I differ—you on the conservation issue.
4. How does 'value education' differ—'value of education'?
5. A timid man is disqualified—romantic ventures.
6. Malpractice in the exams disqualified her—further exam attempts.
7. We would like to put—Michael as our leader.
8. Tell me the truth in stead of putting me—with baseless excuses.
9. Martin, not I, is liable—the lapse.
10. Rukmov's crime makes himself liable—life imprisonment.

IV A

Complete sentences B in the following, making them same/similar in meaning as/to the corresponding sentences A.

1. A. Who can cross the river without being wet?
   B. Nobody . . .
2. A. None upholds culture but the cultivated people.
   B. The cultivated . . . . .
3. A. He has neglected his duty purposefully.
   B. His . . . . .
4. A. If the Principal had not taken a wise decision, the matter would have worsened.
   B. Except for . . . . .
5. A. Don't spell out things in so much detail.
   B. Let . . . . .
6. A. "If I were your boss, I would show you the way.
   B. Simon told Ruth that if . . .
7. A. She disobeyed his orders and that was to his big disappointment.
   B. To . . . .
8. A. Aren't these so-called new ideas old wine in new bottles – a student wonders.
   B. Whether . . .
9. A. As one thinks, so one is.
   B. One is but . . . .
10. A. It is unique that a young child labours for its livelihood.
    B. The labouring of so . . . .

IV B

Fill in the blanks with suitable words:

1. The next flight is bound—Dhaka.
2. Suddenly, the police hit—a splendid idea.
3. It is not fair to look down—the illiterate people.
4. We are glad to congratulate you—your victory.
5. I am afraid I cannot agree—your proposal.
6. My cousin is to answer—his misbehaviour.
7. Normally, the House captains should answer—the warden.
8. The tourists want to call—water source.
9. The health team is about to call—the sick.
10. The Prime Minister calls—a united effort.

V A

1. A. Notwithstanding her good conduct, she was unable to please her father.
   B. Though . . .
2. A. Owing to ill-luck, he met with a bad accident on the eve of his examination
   B. Since . . .
3. A. The first parents disobeyed God and so He punished them.
   B. . . . disobedience.
4. A. You must work sincerely to make good for the lost time.
   B. . . . so that . . .
5. A. Why not search in the bushes; you will find your lost arrow.
   B. Search . . .
6. A. His ego was wounded but he stood firm.
   B. Despite . . .
7. A. The M D of the company saw signs of decline and so he took some precautions.
   B. On . . .
8. A. Martin, being envious of Jack, talked ill of the latter.
   B. Because of . . .
9. A. His growth to prominence was unexpected.
   B. . . . unexpectedly.
10. A. "Will I be capable of reaching your home tomorrow, Jimmi?" Carol wondered.
    B. Carol wondered whether . . .

V B

Fill in the blanks with suitable words:

1. Don't be skeptical; all discussions were—board.
2. I don't know how the hijackers got—board
3. We have full confidence—the school team.
4. The principal has the confidence—the staff.
5. The poor appealed—the District administration through their leader.
6. There was earnest appeal—urgent support from the rich.
7. I know he will meddle—my computer parts.
8. Please leave him alone; don't meddle—his matters.
9. This shop deals—college stationery.
10. This chapter of the book deals—the nature of heat.

VI A

Complete sentences B below, making them similar in meaning to the corresponding Sentences A:

1. A. Even the poorest will work hard if the government supports them sincerely.
   B. Upon . . . . .
2. A. A student will study well if s/he finds the study useful.
   B. Only if . . . .
3. A. When does man win just through muscle power?
   B. One cannot . . .
4. A. Her heart aches deeply.
   B. She has a . . . .
5. A. The teacher enjoyed the poem so well that the students hardly ignored it.
   B. The teacher's . . . . . was too . . . .
6. A. When you reach here, your kids will welcome you.
   B. No sooner . . . .
7. A. Rolling stones don't gather moss.
   B. Those stones . . .
8. A. Helen has as many awards and trophies as her brother has.
   B. Helen does not . . . .
9. A. The river is carrying both friends and foes.
   B. . . . by the river.
10. A. GNH is too strong a vision to ignore.
    B. GNH is so . . .

VI B

Fill in each blank with an appropriate word. Don't copy the sentences:

(a) Many articles from this magazine can be adapted—young readers.
(b) When will you adapt yourself—the spiritual pursuits of this monastery?
(c) The Medical Team had already agreed—an effective project against H1N1.
(d) Who will blindly agree—such a wild proposition?
(e) I cannot do it; the Accounts officer alone has the authority—fund release.
(f) I can assert its destructibility on the authority—past experiences.
(g) Amy bargains—the saleswoman on the cost of a PC.
(h) No person of dignity would bargain—his/her image by accepting bribes.
(i) At length, he turned—to be a well—trained cheat.
(j) It would be embarrassing if the winner of the contest turned—the organizing committee's award.

VII A

Complete sentences B in the following, making them same/similar in meaning as/to the corresponding sentences A.

1. A. Broadcast the sports story next.
   B. Let . . .
2. A. If the Police had not persuaded the teenagers, the latter would have remained drug addicts.
   B. But for . . .
3. A. "If you cast the net here, you will get a lot of fish."
   B. The sage told the fisherman that . . .
4. A. The teachers are worried – Will Shakespeare be removed from the syllabus?
   B. Whether . . .
5. A. The villagers were amused that the head man danced with them.
   B. To the villagers' . . .
6. A. It is encouraging that the problem was solved in a short time.
   B. The solution of the problem in so . . .
7. A. To worry about things beyond one's control is the surest way for sickness.
   B. No other way is . . .
8. A. Who has thought of such an excellent idea?
   B. By whom . . . ?
9. A. None but our Principal supported open-book exams.
   B. The Principal . . .
10. A. Students should develop good habits, or they will go astray.
    B. To prevent . . .

VII B

Complete the sentences below with suitable words:

1. a. The corrupt leader dispensed the jobs—his relatives
   b. New machines are supposed to dispense—the boredom of too much work.
2. a. His flirtations, which the average girl would fall—,are unsafe.
   b. A well-planned scheme is unlikely to fall—.
3. a. The industrious ant has laid—enough for winter.
   b. The new designer will lay—the town.
4. a. To my surprise, the thief made away—five gas cylinders.
   b. The owner made—the thief at least for half a mile.
5. a. Lincoln made up—the spoiled book by hard work..
   b. Great Gurus advise us to make it up—our enemies.

VIII A

Complete sentences B in the following, making them same/similar in meaning as/to the corresponding sentences A.

1. A. The singer practises music too religiously to be distracted.
    B. The singer practises music so . . .
2. A. Raju is a bully today because he, as a student, has been bullied by teachers.
    B. For . . .
3. A. I cannot conform to his ideas, as they have never raised my curiosity.
    B. I have never been . . .
4. A. The whole nation stood relieved upon the arrival of the showers after a decade.
    B. Hardly . . . .
5. A. "Simon, do you by some means hit upon a way out for me?"
    B. Darren asked Simon . . .
6. A. Shed not a drop of blood.
    B. Let . . .
7. A. The downtrodden alone deserve the uplift.
    B. None . . .
8. A. T. S Eliot is harder than I ever fancied.
    B. Never . . .
9. A. Even the emperor nods when Sleep descends.
    B. On . . .
10. A. Did ad hoc activities shake your passion?
    B. . . . . . by ad hoc activities?

VIII B

1. a. We unanimously put—Michael as our leader.
    b. You cannot put me—with silly excuses.
2. a. Nicholas, not I, is liable—the mistake.
    b. her character itself makes her liable—a heavy fine.
3. a. The baby somehow points—the cupboard.
    b. He points—the possible way out of the fix.
4. a. Einstein undoubtedly was genius—science.
    b. Kate has a genius—painting.
5. a. All captains attended the meeting with the exception—Michael.
    b. All agents took exception—cutting down loan rates.

IX A

Complete sentences B in the following, making them same/similar in meaning as/to the corresponding sentences A.

1. A. The man is too cool to be intimidated
   B. The man is so . . .
2. A. Pip was unable to respond to Estella as he had had hard childhood days.
   B. For . . .
3. A. I would oppose the move as the matter was not properly deliberated on.
   B. In the absence of . . .
4. A. The uncle was welcomed warmly as he got down from his car.
   B. Hardly . . . .
5. A. "Emily, did you reach the school early yesterday?"
   B. Amy asked Emily . . .
6. A. Cast off your sad conduct.
   B. Let . . .
7. A. The sweating peasants alone taste their food.
   B. None . . .
8. A. The assignment is harder than I anticipated
   B. Never . . .
9. A. Even a skylark may stop singing at the sight of such sad incidents.
   B. On . . .
10. A. Does the azure sky teach you deep philosophies?
    B. . . . . . by the azure sky?

IX B

1. a. It is but natural that his uncle backed him—in the dispute.
   b. Now, are you backing—? Then , why on earth did you promise to help?
2. a. Everything was discussed and all transactions made—board.
   b. Our first encounter was—board an Indian aircraft.
3. a. I am trying to cut down—drinks.
   b. Please don't cut—; let him continue his talk.
4. a. I never thought he would fall in—my views.
   b. It's so sad that you have fallen—with your brother.
5. a. All were present with the exception—our class teacher.
   b. She took exception—my remarks.

X A

Complete sentences B in the following, making them same/similar in meaning as/to the corresponding sentences A.

1. A. He got angry when he was defeated in the debate.
    B. On . . . .
2. A. Since he had been absent for days, he had to struggle to follow the lesson.
    B. Having . . . .
3. A. He is not so short that he cannot reach the board.
    B. He is not too . . . .
4. A. The harvest will be good though the monsoon failed.
    B. Notwithstanding . . .
5. A. I spoke ill of his father so that his filial love might be aroused.
    B. In order to . . . .
6. A. Can we use the solar lights if electricity fails?
    B. (Use 'electricity failure')
7. A. The more data you have, the readier you become.
    B. Your readiness . . . .
8. A. Wherever she went, she cast calamity around.
    B. (Don't use 'Wherever she went')
9. A. People are amazed that she promptly responded to us.
    B. (Remove either 'amazed' or 'responded' as verbs)
10. A. People watch the sentimental serials; it is a mystery to me.
    B. That . . .

X B

1. Though the meeting took two hours, they agreed—good project.
2. However I try, she just would not agree—his suggestion.
3. Do you plan to complain—the Headquarters?
4. Why not complain—improper sanitation facilities in the house.
5. Some ladies found it difficult to part—their jewels.
6. Come vacation; It is difficult to part—friends.
7. In that lonely hut in the wilderness, he listened—bird songs.
8. My mother listened attentively—the teacher's talk.
9. Victory of any endeavour is a result—planned execution.
10. Driving the people can result—a bad aftertaste.

{**Answers:**

I A.

   1. He asked me whether I was happy with that amount that day.

   2. B. Scarcely did he see the police when he stopped the vehicle.

   3. The box is so heavy that it cannot be lifted.

   4. On seeing his son, Michael rushed to him.

   5. Los Angeles is one of the biggest towns in Bhutan.

   6. You were offered the pen by whom? / The pen was offered to you by whom? (Who were you offered the pen by?)

   7. I don't know the reason for your disappointment.

   8. Everyone knows who composed this music.

   9. He is too stubborn to yield to that temptation.

   10. Your laziness proves this.

I B

   1. with 2. of 3. in 4. to 5. in 6. of 7. on 8. for 9. to 10. on

II A

   1. No other country in the world is as small as Vatican.

   2. She had been given patience by long years of sufferings.

   3. Her sister is calmer than she is.

   4. Can you tell me of the time of his trial.

   5. Corruption is seldom smelt of by his action.

   6. No sooner does my car come than my pet dog barks.

   7. The desire of the dying man was laughed at by the public.

   8. The worsening of our economy was much discussed.

   9. Caesar was praised for his valour by Mark Antony.

   10. My uncle told Benjamin that if he had been older he would not have forgiven him.

II B

   1. to 2. of 3. for 4. to 5. of 6. of 7. on 8. upon 9. for 10. of

III A

   1. On hearing the news, he burst out in tears.

   2. I didn't know the cause of his anger.

   3. Can you tell me the time of his arrival?

   4. All know who wrote this novel.

   5. You were taught grammar by whom?/ Who were you taught grammar by?

   6. The Mayor's speech was loudly cheered by the audience.

   7. She has been given enough courage by circumstances.

   8. Caesar accused of ambition by Brutus.

   9. A happy millionaire has never been heard of . . .

   10. No sooner did he come than he made objections.

III B

1. of 2. to 3. with 4. from 5. for 6. from 7. forward 8. off 9. for 10. to

IV A

1. Nobody can cross the river without being wet.
2. The cultivated people alone uphold culture.
3. His neglect of the duty was purposeful.
4. Except for the Principal's wise decision, the matter would have been worsened.
5. Let not things be spelt out so much in detail.
6. Simon told Ruth that if he had been her boss, he would have shown the way.
7. To his big disappointment, she disobeyed his orders.
8. Whether or not these so-called new ideas are old wine in new bottles is what a student wonders.
9. One is but what one thinks.
10. The laboring of so young a child for its livelihood is unique.

IV B

1. for 2. upon 3. upon 4. on 5. to 6. for 7. to 8. at 9. on 10. for

V A

1. Though she had a good conduct, she was unable to please her father.
2. Since he was unlucky, he met with an accident on the eve of his examinations.
3. The first parents were punished by God for their disobedience.
4. You must work sincerely so that you may make good for the lost time.
5. Search in the bushes so that you will find your lost arrow.
6. Despite his wounded ego, he stood firm.
7. On seeing signs of decline, the M D of the company took some precautions.
8. Because of envy, Martin talked ill of Daniel.
9. He grew to prominence unexpectedly.
10. Carol wondered whether she would be capable of reaching Jimmi's house the following day.

V B

1. above 2. on 3. in 4. of 5. to 6. for 7. with 8. in 9. in 10. with

VI A

1. Upon being sincerely supported by the government, even the poorest will work hard.
2. Only if a student finds the study useful will he study well.
3. One cannot win just through muscle power.
4. She has a deep heart ache.
5. The teacher's enjoyment of the poem was too good for the students to ignore it.
6. No sooner do you reach here than your kids will welcome you.
7. Those stones that roll don't gather moss.
8. Helen does not have more awards and trophies than her brother has.
9. Both friends and foes are being carried by the river.
10. GNH is so strong a vision that it cannot be ignored.

VI B

1. from 2. to 3. upon 4. to 5. for 6. of 7. with 8. away 9. out 10. down

VII A

1. Let the sports story be broadcast next.
2. But for the Police's persuasion, the teenagers would have remained drug addicts.
3. The sage told the fisherman that if they cast the net there, they would get a lot of fish.
4. Whether Shakespeare will be removed from the syllabus is the teachers' worry.
5. To the villagers' amusement, the head man danced with them.
6. The solution of the problem in so short a time is encouraging.
7. No other way is as sure as worrying about things beyond one's control.
8. By whom has such an excellent idea been thought of?
9. The Principal alone supported open-book exams.
10. To prevent students' going astray, they should develop good habits.

VII B

1a. to 1b. with 2a. for 2b. through 3a. up 3b. out 4a. with 4b. after 5a. for 5b. with

VIII A

1. The singer practices music so religiously that s/he cannot be distracted.
2. For having been bullied in his student days by teachers, Raju is a bully today.
3. I have never been curious about his ideas, which I cannot conform to.
4. Hardly did the showers arrive after a decade when the whole nation stood relieved.
5. Darren asked Simon whether he by some means hit upon a way out for him(Darren)
6. Let not a drop of blood be shed.
7. None but the downtrodden deserves the uplift.
8. Never did I fancy that T. S Eliot would be so hard.
9. On the descent of Sleep, even the emperor nods.
10. Was your passion shaken by ad hoc activities?

VIII B

1. a. forward 1. b. of 2. a. for 2. b. to 3.a. to 3. b. out 4.a. in 4. b. for 5. a. of 5. b. to

IX A

1. The man is so cool that he cannot be intimidated
2. For having had hard childhood days, Pip was unable to respond to Estella.
3. In the absence of proper deliberations of the matter, I would oppose the move.
4. Hardly did he get down from his car when the uncle was welcomed.
5. Amy asked Emily whether she had reached the school early the previous day.
6. Let your sad conduct be cast off.
7. None but the sweating peasants taste their food.
8. Never did I anticipate that the assignment would be hard.
9. On seeing such sad incidents, even a skylark may stop singing.
10. Are you taught deep philosophies by the azure sky?

IX B

1.a. up 1. b. out 2. a. 2. b. on 3. a. on 3. b. in 4. a. with 4. b. out 5a. of 5. b. to

X A

1. On being defeated in the debate, he got angry.
2. Having been absent for days, he had to struggle to follow the lesson.
3. He is not too short to reach the board.
4. Notwithstanding the failed monsoon, the harvest will be good.
5. In order to arouse his filial love, I spoke ill of his father.
6. In case of electricity failure, can we use the solar lights?
7. Your readiness depends directly on the amount of data you have.
8. She cast calamity everywhere she went.
9. People are amazed at her prompt response to us.
10. That people watch sentimental serials is a mystery to me.

X B

1. On/upon 2. to 3. to 4. of/ about 5. with 6. from 7. for 8. to 9. of 10. in

----